Ça bouge

Livre de l'étudiant Niveau 1

by **Michael Sedunary**
and **Amanda Rainger**

Ça bouge **Niveau 1**
Written by Michael Sedunary and Amanda Rainger
Illustrated by Bill Wood
Designed by Valerie Sargent

Published by
Accent Educational Publishers Ltd
17 Isbourne Way
Winchcombe
Gloucestershire GL54 5NS
Telephone: (0242) 604466
Fax: (0242) 604480

Ça bouge **Niveau 1**
Student's Book: **ISBN 1 85693 003 3**

Also available in *Ça bouge* Niveau 1:
Teacher's Book: **ISBN 1 85693 004 1**
Class Cassette Pack: **ISBN 1 85693 005 X**
Self-study Cassette: **ISBN 1 85693 006 8**
Workbook: **ISBN 1 85693 007 6**

© CIS Educational Pty Ltd 1988, 1989, 1990, 1991
© Chancerel Publishers Ltd 1989, 1990, 1991
© Accent Educational Publishers Ltd 1990, 1991

All rights reserved. No part of this publication may reproduced, recorded, transmitted or stored in any retrieval system, in any form whatsoever, without the written permission of the copyright holders.

Acknowledgements
Ça bouge was developed and produced by writers, teachers and editors in three countries:

Britain
Chief editor	Amanda Rainger
Contributing editor	Duncan Prowse
Designer	Valerie Sargent
Illustrator	Alan Suttie
Production editor	Liz Woodbridge
Photographers	Jan Chipps
	David Simson
Produced by	Chancerel Publishers Ltd

France
Language Advisors	Liliane Reichenbach
	Flavie Vassor
Educational Advisors	Michel Vassor

The writers and editors would like to express their particular thanks to the staff and students of the *Collège Jean Moulin*, Le Havre, for their enthusistic collaboration.

Australia
Contributors	Gretchen Bennett
	Margaret Gearon
	Elio Guarnuccio
Illustrator	Bill Wood
Photographers	Elio Guarnuccio
	Michael Sedunary
Designer	Josie Semmler
Editor	Helen McBride

Photographs
Cover: David Simson
Air Europe 37; Anglo-Continental 65; Bonbel 6; "Le Boulevard" Hotel Restaurant 109; British Rail International 24, 91; Brittany Ferries 65; "Le Cantorbery" Restaurant 109; Chambourcy 6; Château Camut 6; Château Jalousie 6; J. Chipps/Chancerel 2, 4, 5, 9, 11, 12, 13, 14, 15, 18, 19, 20, 25, 26, 31, 32, 33, 34, 35, 37, 44, 45, 46, 47, 52, 53, 57, 58, 59, 60, 74, 75, 76, 78, 85, 89, 92, 96, 103, 104, 106; Citröen 6; Collège Jean Moulin 104; Confitures Valade 106; Documentation Française 49; Éditions la "goélette" 62, 64; Elio Guarnuccio and Michael Sedunary 4, 23, 26, 48, 50, 51, 59, 61, 62, 63, 64, 67, 77, 82, 83, 90, 93, 105, 108, 109; Hotels Ibis 37; Hoverspeed 25; International Harvest 6; Marie Foodstuffs 6; Michelin Tyre Company 6; Nescafé 106; Nivea 79; Orangina 106; © 1935, 1946, 1961, 1985, Parker Brothers, Division de Kenner Parker toys Inc., Beverley, MA 01915, USA 77; Planète 91; P&O European Ferries 24; Amanda Rainger 10, 25; Tony Rainger 22; Saint-Yorre 6; Sally Ferries 24; Service Photographique de la Réunion des Musées Nationaux 64; David Simson 91; Source Perrier 6; Spectrum Colour Library 64; Tartare Cheese 6; Thé Éléphant 106; Transchannel 65; Yoplait 6. Every effort has been made to trace the copyright holders of all illustrations. The publishers apologise for any omissions and will be pleased to make the necessary arrangements at the first opportunity.

Contents

Introduction ... v

Unité un 1
Salut, bonjour, bonsoir ... 1

Learn how to: ... 2
Greet somebody your own age
Say goodbye to someone
Ask someone their name
Say what your name is
Say who someone else is
Offer someone something
Accept something offered

Ça c'est le français ... 5
Which greeting to use when

Learning about language
Starting out with a good French accent

Le français est partout ... 6
French words all around us
Make a collage of French labels

Unité deux 2
Je suis désolée ... 8

Learn how to: ... 9
Greet adults
Say goodbye to adults
Ask how someone feels
Say how you feel
Apologise

Chanson ... 12
A song to learn and sing

Ça c'est le français ... 13
Saying the right thing

Les sons · Leçon · Les sons ... 13
Pronouncing the French sound **a**

Les prénoms
Is your name on the **calendrier**? ... 14
Choose your French name

Unité trois 3
Toutou et le directeur ... 16

Learn how to: ... 18
Ask who someone is
Say who it is
Count up to 16
Ask how many of something
Say how many
Ask how old someone is
Say how old you are
Describe yourself and others

Ça c'est le français
Check that you know how to say your age and to describe things

Allons en France... ... 24
Take a trip to France or Belgium

Learning about language ... 26
French words you know already
— because they're English!

Les sons · Leçon · Les sons ... 27
Success with a French **u** sound

Unité quatre 4
J'adore l'école ... 28

Learn how to: ... 31
Give descriptions of people
Agree and disagree about people and school
Express your likes and dislikes
Give information about yourself
Ask for information about others

Ça c'est le français ... 36
How to use adjectives to describe people and things

L'Europe et la France ... 37
France — at the centre of Europe.
Practise spelling in French

Les vacances en Grande-Bretagne ... 38
Why do the French come to Britain on holiday?

Learning about language ... 39
How to make learning new words easy

Les sons · Leçon · Les sons ... 39
Tackling the sound **é**

Unité cinq 5
Bobot a tout ... 41

Learn how to: ... 44
Ask what something is
Say what something is
Ask where someone is
Say where something is
Correct someone when they're wrong
Tell people to do things
Ask for things in a shop
Ask how much something costs
Say how much something costs
Say what colour something is
— and train dogs!

Ça c'est le français ... 49
— How to give orders to people

L'Hexagone ... 50
Find your way around France

L'école en France ... 51
The French school system —
could you cope with it?

Les sons · Leçon · Les sons ... 53
How to pronounce **ou** correctly

trois

Contents

Unité six 6

Bon week-end — 54

Learn how to: — 57
Say what you like doing
Say what you're going to do
Ask what someone's going to do
Say what someone's going to do
Ask where people live
Say where you live
Say where other people live
Talk about things you have at home
Invite people to your place

Ça c'est le français — 61
How to talk about your plans

Quatre-vingt-seize heures à Paris — 62
Take a quick trip to the capital of France

Huit raisons de visiter la Grande-Bretagne — 65
Find out what French people look for when they holiday in Britain

Petits poèmes — 66
Poems to read, listen to, learn and write

Learning about language — 67
Reading in French — how to make the most of what you know

Les sons · Leçon · Les sons — 67
The secret of making the French **r** sound

Le Jeu du week-end — 68
Lots of fun with the weekend board game

Unité sept 7

Allons à Paris — 71

Learn how to: — 74
Ask what someone is doing
Say what you're doing
Say what someone else is doing
Identify parts of the body
Identify family members

Ça c'est le français — 79
How the **-er** verbs work

Rendez-vous par ordinateur — 80
Find your ideal friend via a computer questionnaire

La Belle France — 81
More about France's beautiful countryside

Learning about language — 83
How some other languages are related to French

Les sons · Leçon · Les sons — 84
The rhythm of language

Unité huit 8

Le concours — 86

Learn how to: — 89
Talk about the weather
Discuss the seasons
Give the day and the date
Say where you were born
Say what people like doing

Ça c'est le français — 94
A neat way to talk about us

Learning about language — 95
How to make sure you understand what you hear — and what you read

Ici on parle français — 96
French around the world

Les sons · Leçon · Les sons — 97
Follow your nose!

Unité neuf 9

On va au cinéma? — 99

Learn how to: — 103
Talk about food
Say you're hungry and thirsty
Order something to eat and drink
Ask for the bill
Pay the bill
Speak more formally in French

Ça c'est le français — 107
The two ways of saying you
Would you like . . . ?

Baguettes, croissants et crêpes — 108
Tasty snacks to eat in France

Ça fait combien? — 109
And how to pay for them

Learning about language — 110
Using a dictionary

Les sons · Leçon · Les sons — 110
More about talking though your nose!

Appendice — 112

Vocabulaire français-anglais — 113

English-French Vocabulary — 117

iv

quatre

Introduction

ABOUT ÇA BOUGE

There are nine **unités**, or units, in **Ça bouge Niveau 1** - the first level of **Ça bouge**. In (nearly) all of them you will find each of the sections listed below.

UNITÉ UN
Salut, bonjour, bonsoir

Cartoon story

Each cartoon story features an episode in the lives of a group of friends at **le collège Jules Verne** - Jules Verne Secondary School - somewhere in France. There are lots of characters, but the main ones are:

The kids:

Nathalie

Désirée

Sandrine

Paul

Gilles

Roger

The teachers:

Mademoiselle Colbert, French teacher. (Remember, that's the equivalent of your English teacher).

Monsieur Dumas - Maths teacher

Madame Leclerc - PE teacher

Monsieur Ravel - Music teacher

Monsieur Baron - English teacher

Mademoiselle Pappas - History teacher

Monsieur Simon - the Head

The cartoon story is the first thing you'll see in each **unité**. It contains the new words and phrases that you're going to learn and practise. It may also use words that you have already learnt. It's recorded on the cassette, so that you can hear what the people are saying as well as reading the words on the page.

Don't worry if you don't understand every word in the story the first time round. The main thing is to get a general idea of what's happening - and to enjoy the cartoons!

After you've done some work on other pages in the **unité**, your teacher will probably come back to the cartoon story, and you'll be amazed at how much more you understand!

Toutou, Gilles' dog and Debussy, Roger's cat

Introduction

Parlons

Parlons means: Let's talk. Using these pages you can practise speaking French.

The first item on each **Parlons** page is the **photo dialogue**. In this you see some of the main ways of saying things that you're going to practise further down the page. The dialogue is always on tape, so that you can hear and repeat the words just as a French person would say them.

The next item on the **Parlons** page is the **practice** section. At the top of this are the words:

Pour utiliser chaque expression avec chaque dessin/photo, changez les mots en italique.

This means: To use each expression with each drawing/photo, change the words in italics.

The practice section gives you a chance to practise some of the new words and ways of saying things that you have just met in the cartoon story and/or in the photo dialogue.

On each page you'll see a number of boxes, like this:

A Tu t'appelles comment?
ou
Comment t'appelles-tu?

Je m'appelle *Sandrine.*

and a number of pictures: like this:

You can do this exercise on your own, with your teacher, or a friend. Say either of the sentences in the top part of the box (in this example: **Tu t'appelles comment?**). Point to whichever picture you choose and reply using the words in the other half of the box. You repeat the words in ordinary type (in this example, **Je m'appelle**) every time. But according to the picture you have chosen, you change the word(s) *in italics* (in this example *Sandrine*). So if you point to the picture of Gilles, you have to reply, **Je m'appelle *Gilles*.**

vi   six

Introduction

Parlons... avec un(e) partenaire

After you've used the **Parlons** pages to practise each of the new words and sentences you've learnt, you'll want to put them all together. **Parlons avec un(e) partenaire** means: Let's talk with a partner. This will help you have a real French conversation with a partner.

This picture reminds you that one of you should play the part of **A**, while the other is **B**.

| A | Bonjour.
Bonsoir.
Salut. | Tu t'appelles comment?
Comment t'appelles-tu? |

| B | Je m'appelle

Je suis | André.
Laurent.
Colette.
Anne. | Et toi? |

Each box is divided into columns. In this first example there are two. If you are **A** you:
1. choose one of the three words in column 1, for example, **Bonsoir**;
2. then choose one of the two phrases in column 2, for example, **Tu t'appelles comment?**

B then looks at the next box (in which there are three columns) and:
1. chooses a phrase from column 1, for example, **Je m'appelle**;
2. then something from column 2, for example, **Laurent**;
3. then says the phrase in column 3, **Et toi?** You and your partner have just had a conversation in French! Next time swap roles and change the phrases you use.

Parlons... en situation

This means: Let's talk in a (real) situation. This part of each **unité** suggests different situations in which you could use the new language you've learnt, and reminds you of all the things you should be able to say in that situation. Work with a partner or in a group. This time, it's up to you both to think of how to say the things you need.

Imagine what would happen if you were rushing along the corridor and bumped into the Head, knocking him over. As the example shows, you would need to be able to say what your name is, and apologise. Let's hope you can do it better than Désirée!

Ça c'est le français

Ça c'est le français means something like That's the way French works. Before you play a game, you have to learn the rules, and for each game, the rules are different. It's the same when you learn a language. French has its own set of rules, or grammar, which tells you how the language works. As you learn more words and phrases, it helps if you learn the grammar rules for using them correctly. The **Ça c'est le français** section picks up new words and phrases from the **unité** and uses them to explain how parts of the French language work. It's worth reading this page carefully several times. It's a good idea too to go back and look at these sections when you've moved on to later **unités**

sept vii

Introduction

Learning about language

This section has all sorts of interesting information, for example showing you words that are used in both English and French. It also gives you tips to help you to speak French faster and more easily. Again, it's worth reading this section several times and going back to earlier ones from time to time.

Leçon • Les sons • Leçon • Les sons

Les sons are <u>sounds</u> which you will hear in your **Leçon** - <u>lesson</u>, so this section helps you to pronounce French sounds correctly. It's all on Cassette, so you can even take it home and practise it on your own. You could baffle the local English-speaking dogs by saying **ouah! ouah!** to them!

Vocabulaire

In the vocabulary section at the end of the **unité**, you'll find all the new words and phrases you've met in the **unité**. They're divided into separate groups to help you refer to them and to learn them more easily. There are also French-English and English-French wordlists at the end of the book which contain all the words you've met in the book.

Quel progrès!

Tells you <u>What progress!</u> you're making by reminding you of all the useful new things you've learnt in the **unité**. Use it as a checklist, to make sure you've really learnt them properly. No cheating mind!

Regardez maintenant les fiches...

This sign tells you <u>Now you can look at one or more worksheets</u>. You'll see a sign like this after most sections and on almost every page of the **unité**, reminding you that now you've studied that page you're ready to see how much you've learnt by tackling a follow-up activity. This might involve listening, speaking, reading or writing - or a mixture of these. The signs at the top of each **fiche** will tell you what kind of activity it is and what you will need. For example:

Listening to the tape and highlighting answers on the worksheet

Looking in the Student's Book for your answer, then writing it on the worksheet.

The **fiches** are divided into three groups.
* One-star activities - for people who have just started, or need a little more practice.
** Two-star, or core, activities - suitable for most people most of the time.
*** Three-star activities - for people who feel they can manage something a little more complicated.

viii

huit

UNITÉ UN
Salut, bonjour, bonsoir

Parlons

Série Un

1. Comment t'appelles-tu?
2. Je m'appelle Pierre.
3. Salut, Pierre. Je suis Mathieu.
4. Bonjour, Mathieu.

Pour utiliser chaque expression avec chaque dessin, changez les mots en italique.

A Tu t'appelles comment?
   ou
   Comment t'appelles-tu?

   Je m'appelle *Sandrine.*

B Ah, voilà *Roger.*
   ou
   Je suis *Roger.*

   Salut, *Roger.*
   ou
   Bonjour, *Roger.*

1

2

3

4

5

6

Regardez maintenant: les fiches B1 et B2

2 deux

Unité un

Parlons

Série Deux

Pour utiliser chaque expression avec chaque dessin, changez les mots en italique.

A *Bonsoir!*

B *Bonne nuit, Paul.*

Regardez maintenant: la fiche C1

Parlons... avec un(e) partenaire

"Moi, je suis **A**. Toi, tu es **B**."

"D'accord."

| A | Bonjour. Bonsoir. Salut. | Tu t'appelles comment? Comment t'appelles-tu? |

| B | Je m'appelle / Je suis | André. Laurent. Colette. Anne. | Et toi? |

| A | Je m'appelle / Je suis | René. Richard. Yvonne. Agnès. |

"Moi, je suis Jeanne d'Arc. Tu t'appelles comment?"

| B | Salut, Bonsoir, Bonjour, | René. Richard. Yvonne. Agnès. |

Parlons... en situation

INTRODUCING YOURSELF

This is your first day at a new school. You don't know the people sitting around you, so introduce yourself to each of them. Ask each person's name. Each one must reply. Once you have found out the names of some other people, you can point them out to the person you are speaking to.

"Je m'appelle Martin. Comment t'appelles-tu?"

"Moi, je suis Valérie."

"Et voilà Sébastien."

"Ah, Sébastien. Merci, Martin. Au revoir."

Regardez maintenant: les fiches D1 et D2

4 quatre — Unité un

Ça c'est le français

1 GREETING PEOPLE
What greeting you use depends on who you're speaking to. (You wouldn't always use hi! in English, would you?) The table on the right shows what to use.

2 SAYING GOODBYE
Au revoir! This is the commonest way of saying goodbye. If you're expecting to see the other person soon, you can say **à bientôt**. When you're off to bed, say **bonne nuit**.

Time	People you know well	People you don't know well
During the day (roughly when we'd say Good morning or Good afternoon)	**Salut** or **Bonjour**	**Bonjour** (not **Salut**)
During the evening	**Salut** or **Bonsoir**	**Bonsoir** (not **Salut**)

Regardez maintenant: les fiches E1 et E2

Learning about language

In the BBC TV series **Allô Allô,** the French people speak English with a strong French accent. Well, French TV has also shown the programme, and there the English people speak French with a strong English accent.

However, when you're speaking French, you'll want to sound as French as possible. To do that, you'll have to practise imitating French sounds. Don't try to work out the sounds from the way words are written. Get into the habit of listening and imitating without looking at your book.

You are used to forming your mouth (lips, tongue and teeth) to make the sounds we need in English. So pronouncing French correctly may sound and feel strange at first, but this is a good sign! You're probably getting it right!

Unité un · cinq 5

Le français est partout

Le français est partout - French is all around us. Sometimes we are so used to the name of the product that we don't actually realise that it's French.
- Can you name three brands of French car that we can buy here?
- Why not make a collage like the one above, to show that **le français est partout**?
- By the way, do you know how to pronounce the word **collage**? (If you don't, ask your teacher.) It's not pronounced as you might expect, because in fact it's a French word.
- Can you find out its original meaning?

Vocabulaire

C'EST BIEN LE MOT

et	and
merci	thank you
voilà	there (it) is

EXPRESSIONS UTILES

je m'appelle	my name is
je suis	I am
tu t'appelles comment?	what's your name?

SALUTATIONS

bonjour	hello, good morning
bonsoir	hello, good evening
salut	hi!
à bientôt	see you soon
au revoir	goodbye
bonne nuit	goodnight

Regardez maintenant: les fiches F1 et F2

Quel progrès!

Félicitations! You are now able to use your French to do the following things:

- greet somebody your own age
- say goodbye to them
- ask someone their name
- say what your name is
- say who you are
- say who someone else is
- offer someone something
- accept something that's offered to you

Unité un
sept 7

UNITÉ DEUX
Je suis désolée

Parlons

Série Un

1. Bonsoir, monsieur.
2. Bonsoir, madame.

Pour utiliser chaque expression avec chaque photo, changez les mots en italique.

1 Monsieur Dumas

2 Madame Robert

3 Mademoiselle Roche

6 Monsieur Vassor

A Je m'appelle *Monsieur Vassor*.
   Je suis *Mademoiselle Roche*.

B Ah, voilà *Madame Robert*!

   Bonjour, *monsieur*.
        ou
   Bonsoir, *madame*.

4 Monsieur Étienne

5 Monsieur Bertrand

Regardez maintenant: la fiche B1

Unité deux

neuf 9

Parlons

Série Deux

¹ Ça va, Cyril?

² Ça va très bien, merci!

Pour utiliser chaque expression avec chaque dessin, changez les mots en italique.

1 Ça va très bien, merci.

2 Pas mal.

Ça va, *Gilles*?
ou
Comment ça va, *Gilles*?

Pas mal.

3 Ça va bien.

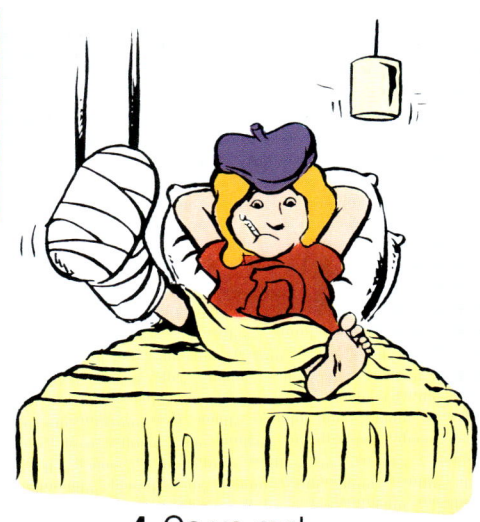

4 Ça va mal.

Regardez maintenant: les fiches C1 et C2

10 dix

Unité deux

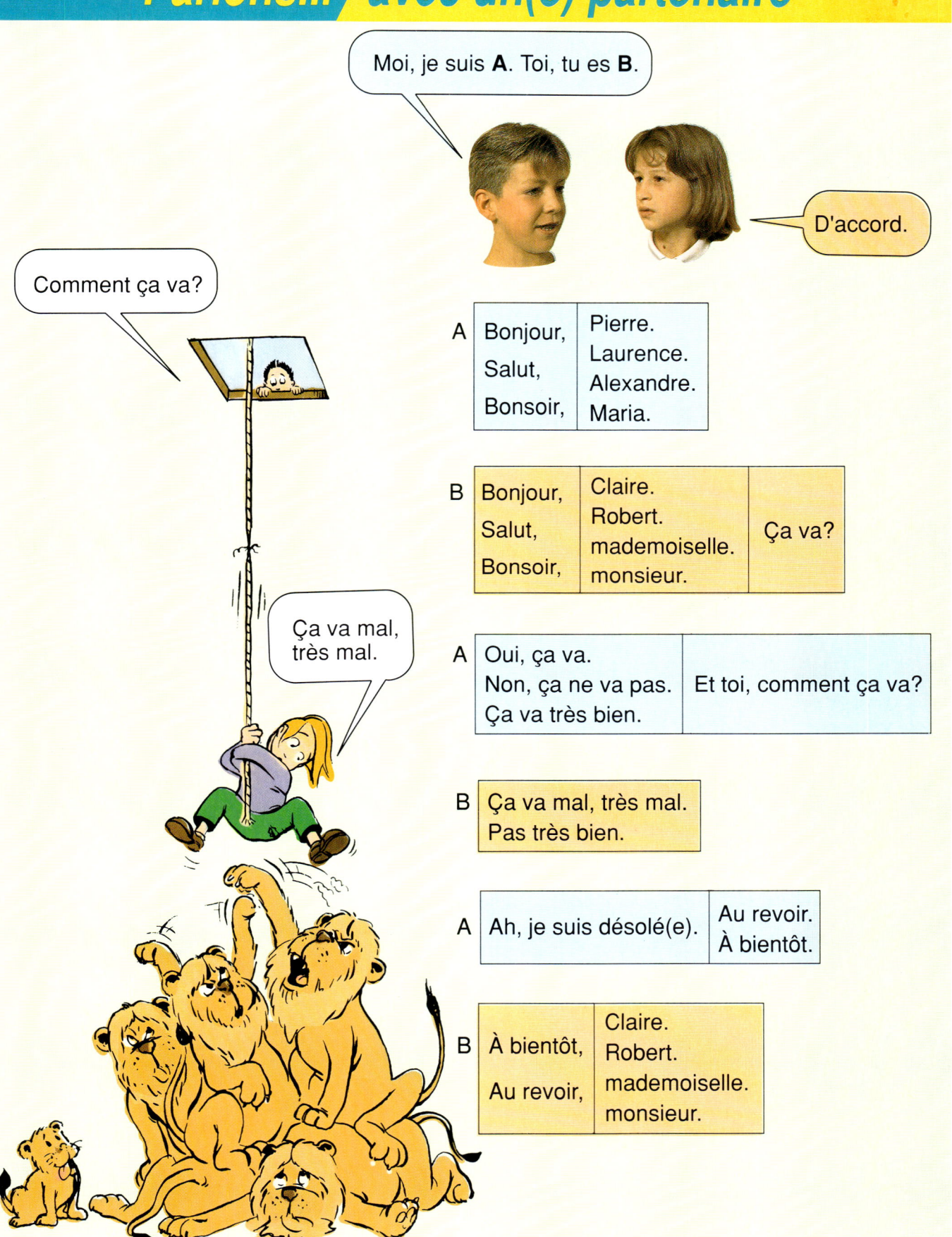

Parlons... en situation

Go over to some people in your class, and greet them by name. Then find out how they are. If they're polite, they'll ask you how you are, and you can say exactly how you feel.

Say goodbye. Don't forget to tell the other person you'll see them later.

Regardez maintenant: la fiche D1

Chanson

Salut, bonjour, bonsoir

Salut, bonjour, bonsoir,
Bonjour, salut, ça va?
Ça va très bien, et toi?
Ah oui, ça va, ça va.

Bonsoir, bonjour, salut,
Et comment t'appelles-tu?
Je m'appelle Laurent,
Et tu t'appelles comment?

Moi, je suis Chantal.
Et ça va mal, très mal.
Salut, Chantal, bonsoir.
Au revoir, Laurent, au revoir.

Ça c'est le français

1 APOLOGISING

Pardon! This is a simple way of making a quick apology for something minor, such as brushing against someone. When you want to sound a little more upset - you may have hurt someone or heard some bad news - you can say **je suis désolé(e).**

2 ASKING HOW PEOPLE ARE

When you greet friends using **salut**, you usually add **ça va?** to ask if they are all right.

Here are some common replies:

Oui, ça va.	Yes, things are fine.
Ça va bien, merci.	I'm well, thanks.
Non, ça ne va pas.	Things are not going well.

You can also ask, **comment ça va?** meaning how are things?

Here are some common replies:

Très bien, merci.	Very well, thanks.
Pas mal.	Not bad.
Ça va mal.	Things are going badly.

3 BONJOUR, MONSIEUR/MADAME

French people tend to be more formal than we are in English. So, for example, in a shop, where we might say good morning only, French people would say **bonjour, monsieur** or **bonjour, madame**.

Leçon · Les sons · Leçon · Les sons · Leçon

When you are pronouncing Nathalie's name in French you have to make an effort to get the right French sound, especially for the **a**. Make sure you don't use the sound southern English speakers use in words like cat. The French **a** sound is more like the u sound people in the south use in words like cut and butter. Use your best southern English accent to say,

Cut the butter, Mum!

Now use your best French accent to say,

Le chat, Nathalie, le chat.

Notice that you pronounce both **a**'s in Nathalie's name in the same way. Use the same short **a** sound to pronounce the following French expressions.

**Ça va mal, très mal.
Pas mal, Annie, pas mal.**

Unité deux treize 13

Les prénoms

BONNE FÊTE!

In France, if you happen to have the same name as a Catholic saint, you have a special name day, or **fête**, which you share with that saint. Is your name Anthony, Jacqueline, or Andrew, for instance? If you can find your name, or a version of it, on the **calendrier** then you have a **fête** too.

JANVIER	FÉVRIER	MARS	AVRIL	MAI	JUIN	JUILLET	AOÛT	SEPTEMBRE	OCTOBRE	NOVEMBRE	DÉCEMBRE
1 —	1 Ella	1 Aubin	1 Hugues	1 —	1 Justin	1 Thierry	1 Alphonse	1 Gilles	1 Thérèse	1 —	1 Florence
2 Basile	2 —	2 Charles	2 Sandrine	2 Boris	2 Blandine	2 Martinien	2 Julien	2 Ingrid	2 Léger	2 —	2 Viviane
3 Geneviève	3 Blaise	3 Guénolé	3 Richard	3 Philippe, Jacques	3 Kévin	3 Thomas	3 Lydie	3 Grégoire	3 Gérard	3 Hubert	3 Xavier
4 Odilon	4 Véronique	4 Casimir	4 Isidore	4 Sylvain	4 Clotilde	4 Florent	4 Jean-Marie	4 Rosalie	4 François	4 Charles	4 Barbara
5 Edouard	5 Agathe	5 Olive	5 Irène	5 Judith	5 Igor	5 Antoine	5 Abel	5 Raïssa	5 Fleur	5 Sylvie	5 Gérald
6 Mélaine	6 Gaston	6 Colette	6 Marcellin	6 Prudence	6 Norbert	6 Marietta	6 —	6 Bertrand	6 Bruno	6 Bertille	6 Nicolas
7 Raymond	7 Eugénie	7 Félicité	7 Jean-Baptiste	7 Gisèle	7 Gilbert	7 Raoul	7 Gaétan	7 Reine	7 Serge	7 Carine	7 Ambroise
8 Lucien	8 Jacqueline	8 Jean	8 Julie	8 —	8 Médard	8 Thibaut	8 Dominique	8 —	8 Pélagie	8 Geoffroy	8 —
9 Alix	9 Apolline	9 Françoise	9 Gautier	9 Pacôme	9 Diane	9 Amandine	9 Amour	9 Alain	9 Denis	9 Théodore	9 —
10 Guillaume	10 Arnaud	10 Vivien	10 Fulbert	10 Solange	10 Landry	10 Ulrich	10 Laurent	10 Inès	10 Ghislain	10 Léon	10 Romaric
11 Paulin	11 —	11 Rosine	11 Stanislas	11 Estelle	11 Barnabé	11 Benoît	11 Claire	11 Adelphe	11 Firmin	11 —	11 Daniel
12 Tatiana	12 Félix	12 Justine	12 Jules	12 Achille	12 Guy	12 Olivier	12 Clarisse	12 Apollinaire	12 Wilfried	12 Christian	12 Jeanne
13 Yvette	13 Béatrice	13 Rodrigue	13 Ida	13 Rolande	13 Antoine	13 Henri, Joël	13 Hippolyte	13 Aimé	13 Géraud	13 Brice	13 Lucie
14 Nina	14 Valentin	14 Mathilde	14 Maxime	14 Matthias	14 Elisée	14 —	14 Evrard	14 —	14 Juste	14 Sidoine	14 Odile
15 Rémi	15 Claude	15 Louise	15 Paterne	15 Denise	15 Germaine	15 Donald	15 —	15 Roland	15 Thérèse	15 Albert	15 Ninon
16 Marcel	16 Julienne	16 Bénédicte	16 Benoît	16 Honoré	16 Régis	16 Carmel	16 Armel	16 Edith	16 Edwige	16 Marguerite	16 Alice
17 Roseline	17 Alexis	17 Patrice	17 Anicet	17 Pascal	17 Hervé	17 Charlotte	17 Hyacinthe	17 Renaud	17 Baudouin	17 Elisabeth	17 Gaël
18 Prisca	18 Bernardette	18 Cyrille	18 Parfait	18 Eric	18 Léonce	18 Frédéric	18 Hélène	18 Nadège	18 Luc	18 Aude	18 Gatien
19 Marius	19 Gabin	19 Joseph	19 Emma	19 Yves	19 Romuald	19 Arsène	19 Jean	19 Emilie	19 René	19 Tanguy	19 Urbain
20 Sébastien	20 Aimée	20 Herbert	20 Odette	20 Bernardin	20 Silvère	20 Marina	20 Bernard	20 Davy	20 Adeline	20 Edmond	20 Abraham
21 Agnès	21 Damien	21 Clémence	21 Anselme	21 Constantin	21 —	21 Victor	21 Christophe	21 Matthieu	21 Céline	21 —	21 Pierre
22 Vincent	22 Isabelle	22 Léa	22 Alexandre	22 Emile	22 Alban	22 Marie-Madeleine	22 Fabrice	22 Maurice	22 Élodie	22 Cécile	22 —
23 Barnard	23 Lazare	23 Victorien	23 Georges	23 Didier	23 Audrey	23 Brigitte	23 Rose	23 —	23 Jean	23 Clément	23 Armand
24 François	24 Modeste	24 Catherine	24 Fidèle	24 Donatien	24 Jean-Baptiste	24 Christine	24 Barthélemy	24 Thècle	24 Florentin	24 Flora	24 Adèle
25 Paul	25 Roméo	25 —	25 Marc	25 Sophie	25 Prosper	25 Jacques	25 Louis	25 Hermann	25 Crépin	25 Catherine	25 Noël
26 Paule	26 Nestor	26 Larissa	26 Alida	26 Bérenger	26 Anthelme	26 Anne, Joachim	26 Natacha	26 Côme, Damien	26 Dimitri	26 Delphine	26 Etienne
27 Angèle	27 Honorine	27 Habib	27 Zita	27 Augustin	27 Fernand	27 Nathalie	27 Monique	27 Vincent	27 Emeline	27 Séverin	27 Jean
28 Thomas	28 Romain	28 Gontran	28 Valérie	28 Germain	28 Irénée	28 Samson	28 Augustin	28 Venceslas	28 Simon, Jude	28 Jacques	28 —
29 Gildas	29 Auguste	29 Gwladys	29 Catherine	29 Aymard	29 Pierre, Paul	29 Marthe	29 Sabine	29 Michel	29 Narcisse	29 Saturnin	29 David
30 Martine		30 Amédée	30 Robert	30 Ferdinand	30 Martial	30 Juliette	30 Fiacre	30 Jérôme	30 Bienvenue	30 André	30 Roger
31 Marcelle		31 Benjamin		31 —		31 Ignace	31 Aristide		31 Quentin		31 Sylvestre

TU T'APPELLES COMMENT?

Just as young people in Britain don't always have traditional English names, French children have a mixture of names too. The list below has been taken from a French teenage magazine and shows names which are popular in France at the moment. As you can see, English names are very fashionable!

Jérémie, Nicola, Magalie, Steve, Stéphanie, Habib, Sonia, Francis, Madonna, Franck, Sandra, Anthony, Marjorie, Hakim, Latifa, Stéphane, Shéhérazade, Yann

Moi, je suis Ahmed.

Je m'appelle Aurélie.

Je suis Grégory.

JE SUIS...

Anyway, now that you are a student of French, you could if you like choose a French **prénom**. You might want to find the nearest equivalent to your own name (ask your teacher if there is one) or you might decide to take on a totally new French identity.

Vocabulaire

C'EST BIEN LE MOT!

aïe!	ouch!
madame (Mme)	madam, Mrs
mademoiselle (Mlle)	Miss
monsieur (M)	sir, Mr
pardon	excuse me, sorry
très	very

"Ça va, madame?"

"Ça va très bien, merci."

"Ça va, David?"

"Ça va mal, très mal!"

EXPRESSIONS UTILES

ça va	things are all right
ça va?	how are you?
comment ça va?	how's it going?
ça va bien	I'm fine
ça va très bien	I'm very well
ça va mal	things are going badly
pas mal	not bad
pas très bien	not very well
ça (ne) va pas	things aren't going well
je suis désolé(e)	I'm sorry

Regardez maintenant: les fiches E1, E2 et E3

Quel progrès!

Félicitations! You are now able to use your French to do the following things:

- greet adults
- say goodbye to them
- ask how someone feels
- say how you feel
- apologise

Unité deux　　　　　　　　　　　　　　　　　　quinze ■ 15

UNITÉ TROIS
Toutou et le directeur

Parlons

Série Un

1. Qui est-ce?
2. C'est le Directeur.
3. Il s'appelle comment?
4. Il s'appelle Monsieur Vassor.

Pour utiliser chaque expression avec chaque photo, changez les mots en italique.

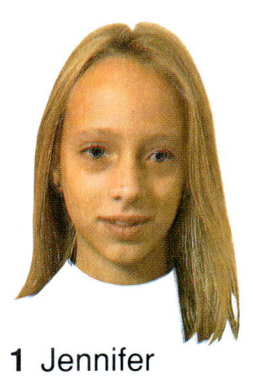

1 Jennifer

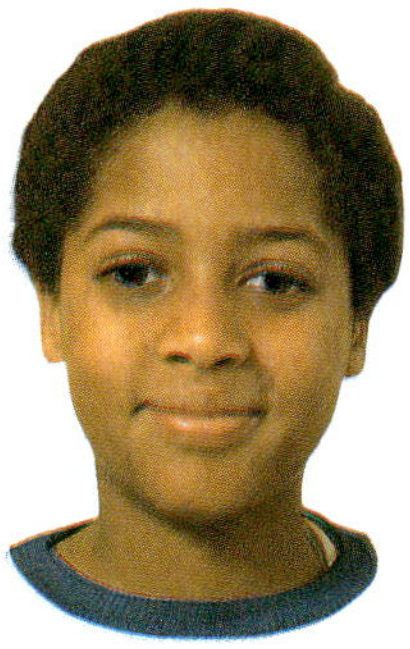

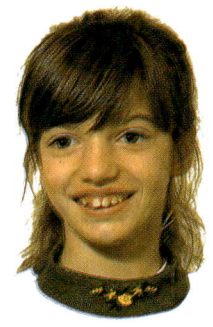

2 Éric

3 Valérie

A	Qui est-ce? ou C'est qui?	B	*Il* s'appelle comment?
	C'est *Valérie*.		*Il* s'appelle *Éric*.

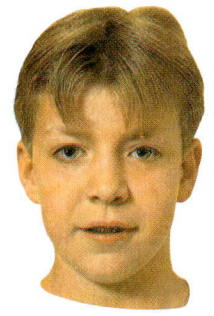

6 Alexandre

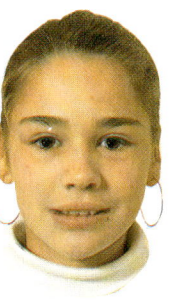

5 Aurélie

4 Jérémie

Regardez maintenant: les fiches B1 et B2

dix-huit

Unité trois

Parlons

Série Deux

...combien de chevaux? Comptons! Un, deux, trois, quatre, cinq, six, sept, huit, neuf, dix, onze, douze, treize, quatorze, quinze...seize...où est le numéro seize? Ah! C'est le Fantôme!

Call the numbers in the order they finish.
Numéro onze...numéro huit...numéro sept...

Pour utiliser l'expression avec chaque cheval, changez les mots en italique.

Le numéro *un*, il s'appelle comment?

Il s'appelle *Directeur*.

LES CONCURRENTS

1. Directeur
2. À Bientôt
3. Élégant
4. Catastrophe
5. Salut Sylvie
6. Très Riche
7. Merci Beaucoup
8. Petit Pierre
9. Pompidou
10. La Belle France
11. Ça Bouge
12. Monsieur Méchant
13. Pas Mal
14. Grand Champion
15. Bonsoir Paris
16. Le Fantôme

Regardez maintenant: les fiches C1, C2, C3, C4 et C5

Unité trois

dix-neuf 19

Parlons

Série Trois

1. J'ai treize ans. Et toi, quel âge as-tu?
2. J'ai douze ans.
3. Je suis grande... intelligente... élégante... et marrante.
4. Je suis petit... intelligent... et content!

Pour utiliser chaque expression avec chaque dessin, changez les mots en italique.

Sandrine
12
grande, intelligente

A Tu as quel âge, *Nathalie*?
ou
Quel âge as-tu, *Nathalie*?

J'ai *onze* ans.

B Je suis *petit(e)*.
Oui, tu es très *petit(e)*.

C Je suis *intelligent(e)*.
C'est *Paul*.

D Je m'appelle *Désirée* et je suis *petite*.
Je m'appelle *Roger* et je suis *petit*.

Roger
12
petit, élégant

Désirée
12
petite, marrante

Paul
12
intelligent, content

Nathalie
11
élégante, contente

Regardez maintenant: les fiches D1, D2 et D3

vingt — Unité trois

Parlons... avec un(e) partenaire

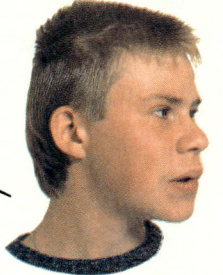

Moi, je suis **A**. Toi, tu es **B**.

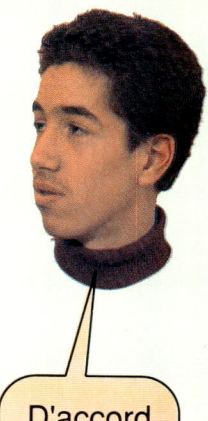

D'accord.

A	Bonjour.	Comment ça va?
	Salut!	Ça va?

B	Salut!	Oui, ça va.	Je suis	André.	Et toi?
	Bonjour.	Ça va bien, merci.	Je m'appelle	Laurent.	
		Ça va très bien.		Colette.	
				Anne.	

A	Moi?	Je m'appelle	Claire.
		Je suis	Claudine.
			Marcel.
			Guy.

B	Mais, tu es	grand(e).	Tu as quel âge?
		petit(e).	Quel âge as-tu?

A	J'ai	onze	ans. Et toi?
		douze	
		treize	
		quatorze	

B	Moi, j'ai	douze	ans.
		treize	
		quatorze	

Qui est-ce?

You see a man coming across the playground.

| A | Il s'appelle comment? |

B	C'est	Monsieur Simon.	
		Monsieur le Directeur.	Vite! La classe de français.
		le Directeur.	

A	Ah oui, la classe de français.	Au revoir.
		À bientôt.

B	Au revoir!
	À bientôt!

Regardez maintenant: les fiches E1 et E2

Unité trois — vingt et un — 21

Parlons... en situation

VITE, LA CLASSE DE MATHS!

You're tearing along the corridor, late for the maths class, when you bump into the Head of the school. You apologise immediately.

The Head then wants to know more about you - your name and age. After having a good look at you she or he comments on your appearance, and also asks a couple of questions to find out a little about your personality.

For example, she or he may ask, **Tu es content(e)?** to which you might answer, **Ah oui, monsieur/mademoiselle/ madame, je suis content(e).**

Then suddenly you both remember the maths class and you rush off to it.

LES PHOTOS

You are looking at some photos brought in by a classmate.

Some were taken years ago and you ask how old your classmate is in the photo, and comment on how they look. You can also ask who the other people in the photos are.

Now it's your turn to show an old photo or two!

Regardez maintenant: les fiches F1 et F2

Unité trois

Ça c'est le français

1 WHO'S THAT?

If you want to ask who someone is, you say
Qui est-ce?

Another way of asking the same question in a more casual way is to say **C'est qui?** This is a useful expression to show that you are really puzzled.

If you want to know someone's name in French, you can say
Il/Elle s'appelle comment?
You could also say
Comment s'appelle-t-il? or
Comment s'appelle-t-elle? (Notice that to make the expression easier to pronounce you have to put an extra **-t-** in if you say it this way round.)

3 DESCRIBING YOURSELF AND OTHERS

The following adjectives are useful when you are talking about yourself or about other people.

grand(e)	tall, big
petit(e)	little, short
content(e)	happy
marrant(e)*	funny
intelligent(e)	intelligent
élégant(e)	elegant

* **Marrant** is a colloquial French word. This means it is used only in casual conversation.

Je suis intelligent(e).	I am intelligent.
Je suis content(e).	I am happy.
Tu es très marrant(e).	You are very funny.
Tu es petit(e).	You are small.

The adjectives in this list (and lots of others, too) have the final **-e** when they refer to a female. In this case you pronounce the final consonant.

4 ME AND YOU

Sometimes you can use the words **moi** and **toi** to make it perfectly clear who you are referring to in your questions and answers.

e.g. **Et toi, tu as quel âge?**
How old are you?
Moi, j'ai quatorze ans.
I'm fourteen.

In these sentences **moi** and **toi** don't have a separate meaning. They just make what you're saying sound stronger and clearer.

Qui est-ce?

C'est Napoléon Bonaparte.

2 AGE

To ask someone's age in French you can choose between two questions.
Tu as quel âge? or **Quel âge as-tu?**
If someone asks you that question you answer, **J'ai...ans.**

When you are giving your age you can't just use a number, you must always add **ans**.

e.g. **J'ai treize ans.** I am thirteen.

Moi, j'ai seize ans.

Regardez maintenant: la fiche G1

Unité trois — vingt-trois 23

Allons en France...

Wherever you live in the British Isles, two of the nearest foreign countries to your home will be **la France** or **la Belgique.** You know that they speak French in France, but did you know that Belgium is one of the other countries where French is spoken?

To get to France or Belgium you can travel by train, coach or car (and ferry, if you're from Ireland) to a port on the English coast, and then take a boat or hovercraft across the sea. Of course, you might use the Channel Tunnel. Or you can take a plane all the way.

The maps show just a few of the routes you can take from different ports and airports in the British Isles to places in France and Belgium; and the route of the new Channel Tunnel.

Par avion - by air

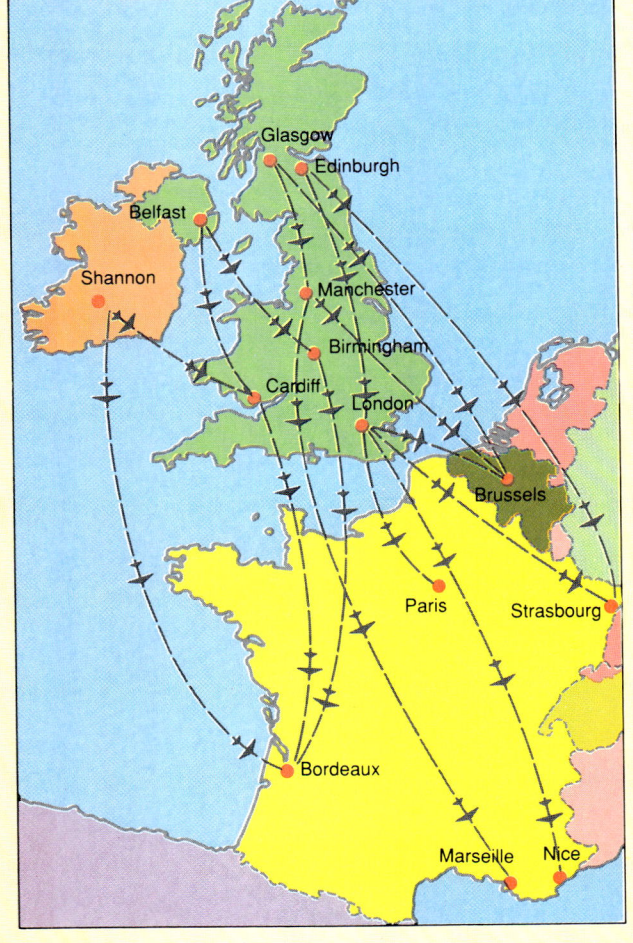

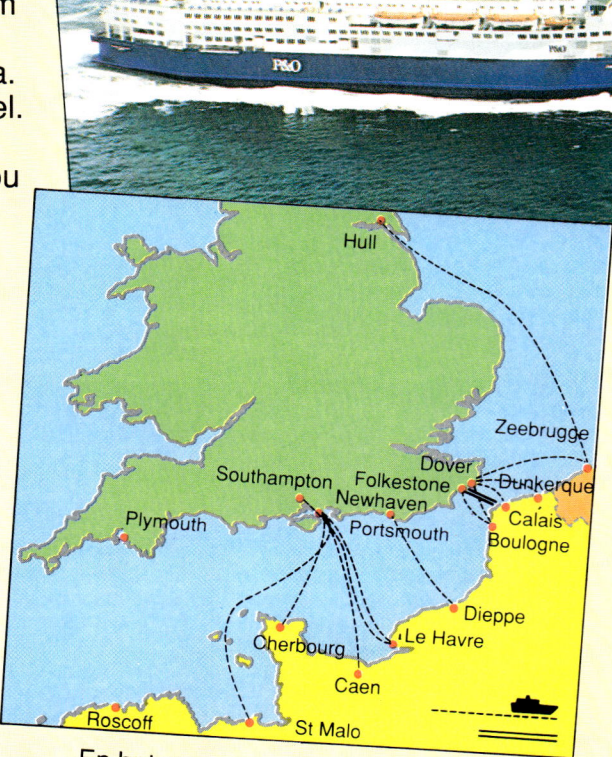

En bateau ou par le Tunnel - by boat or via the Tunnel

LE VOYAGE

Imagine that you are planning a three-day trip to France or Belgium. Here are some of the things that you need to work out before you leave.

- **Avec qui?** Who will you travel with (family, youth group, school)?

- **Comment?** - How are you going to travel (plane, car/coach/train + boat/Tunnel)?

- **Par où?** - Which route will you take?

24 vingt-quatre   Unité trois

...ou en Belgique!

- **Combien de temps?** - How long will the trip take you? You can work it out roughly. A modern jet can average about 500 miles per hour. A car or coach averages about 50 m.p.h. The boat crossing from England to France takes between 1 and 7 hours depending on which route you take. Check your answer with someone who has been there.

- **C'est combien?** - How much will it cost? Can you really afford to go? (There might be some special offers you could take up.) Which is the cheapest way to travel?

- **Les papiers** - What travel documents will you need before you leave? What do you have to do to get them?

- **L'argent** - Money. You won't be using British money when you get there. What will you do about changing your money? How much is a pound worth in French or Belgian money?

You have £40 to spend. How much is that in French money?

- **Le téléphone** - You'll have to ring home when you get there, to say you've arrived. You call at 7.00pm local time. At what time will the phone ring at home?

- **Quel cadeau?** - What present? You want to buy a good quality, typically French or Belgian product as a present for someone at home. What will you buy? Where will you get it?

Unité trois   vingt-cinq   25

Learning about language

Not only are we surrounded by French products in Britain, but if you keep your eyes and ears open you will realise that **le français est partout** - the French language is all around us too.

- What do we call an exclusive little shop specialising in fashionable clothing?
- What word do we use for the uniformed driver of a limousine?
- While out for the day you feel like a cup of tea and a sandwich, your friend wants a coke and some egg and chips. Where do you go?

When it comes to **cuisine** we are bombarded by French words.

- Ask someone at home to explain the following terms: **purée, sauté, soufflé, pâté.**
- Look in your local supermarket for a **quiche** or some **croissants.**

J'aime le fast food.

Moi, je préfère un sandwich.

Why do you think so many French words to do with cooking have come into our language? We have repaid the French by lending them lots of words to do with casual, high-speed, modern living.

J'ai deux tickets pour le match ce weekend.

Je n'aime pas le football. Je préfère le jogging.

Fashion magazines might show that French **couture** is **à la mode**, but for certain fashions it's the English language that supplies the words. **Au club, je porte toujours un jean et un T-shirt.**

Moi, je porte un jean et un pullover!

Et moi, des baskets et un T-shirt.

Many of the words that the French borrow from English seem to have something to do with **le sport** and other recreations such as **le camping.** Why would this be so?

The fact that the French and English have borrowed so heavily from each other is a sign that the two cultures have always been interested in each other. Now, as a student of French, you can share in that interest and build on all those words that you already know.

UNE IDÉE

Pin up a large sheet of paper in your classroom and keep two lists of words going for a whole year: one of French words used in English, the other of words used in French which are borrowed from English.

Here are some to start with. **Allez-y!**

boutique	**le club**
chauffeur	**le camping**
souvenir	**un jean**
crêpe	**le football**

Vocabulaire

C'EST BIEN LE MOT

le cheval	horse
la classe	class
combien?	how many?
le directeur	head of school
elle	she
le français	French
il	he
le, la, les	the
maintenant	now
mais	but
les maths	maths
non	no
la photo	photo

EXPRESSIONS UTILES

mon Dieu!	my goodness
ça alors!	you don't say! (when you're surprised)
c'est	it is, that is
il/elle s'appelle	his/her name is
merci beaucoup	thank you very much
ouah!	woof!
quelle catastrophe!	what a disaster!
quel âge as-tu?	how old are you?
j'ai ...ans	I'm...years old
qui est-ce?	who is it?
vite!	hurry! quickly!

ADJECTIFS

content(e)	happy	marrant(e)	funny
élégant(e)	elegant	méchant(e)	naughty, bad
grand(e)	tall, big	petit(e)	little, short
intelligent(e)	intelligent		

Leçon • Les sons • Leçon • Les sons • Leçon

One sound you must make a special effort with is the French **u**. It is not like any other sound we make when we are speaking English. It is a much thinner, more piercing sound. To get it, try forming your lips to say <u>oo</u>, leave your lips in that position, then say <u>ee</u>.

To get the sound of English out of your system, say, Are you true blue too?

Now practise the French **u** by repeating the following expressions.

Salut Luc. Quel âge as-tu?
Numéro trois.

Quel progrès!

Bravo! You are now able to use your French to do these things:

- ask who it is
- say who it is
- count up to 16
- ask how many
- say how many
- ask how old someone is
- say how old you are
- describe yourself and other people

Regardez maintenant:
les fiches H1, H2, H3 et H4

Unité trois vingt-sept 27

UNITÉ QUATRE
J'adore l'école

7. Et voilà mademoiselle Colbert, professeur de français.
— Elle est petite.
— Oui, et elle est belle.

8. Elle n'est pas belle, elle est moche.

9. Silence! Silence! Asseyez-vous, s'il vous plaît.

10. Mais monsieur Dumas est beau.
— Hmm.

11. Oh, il est chouette. Il a quel âge...vingt, vingt et un?
— Il a vingt-quatre ans, je crois.

Unité quatre   vingt-neuf   29

12. — Mais, où est monsieur Ravel?
— Ah oui, voici le professeur de musique, Monsieur Ravel.

13. — Salut, bonjour, bonsoir.
— Oh zut! Ça suffit.

14. — C'est super, la chanson.
— Oui, ça bouge! J'aime bien monsieur Ravel. Il est formidable.
— Formidable? Il est fou. Moi, je déteste le rock. J'adore la musique classique.

15. — Quel casse-pieds!

16. — Et maintenant, voici Nathalie avec la chanson, *J'adore l'école.*

17. *J'adore l'école, j'aime l'école,*
L'école est pour toujours,
J'aime l'école, j'adore l'école,
L'école est mon amour.
— Beurk! C'est le chouchou.

18. — Merci, Nathalie. Et maintenant, tous ensemble.

19. *C'est une moche école,*
c'est une folle école,
L'école est pour Toutou,
C'est une moche école,
c'est une folle école,
L'école est pour les fous.

Regardez maintenant: les fiches A1 et A2.

30 trente — Unité quatre

Parlons

Série Un

1. Il est beau, Little Bob.
2. Oui, il est très beau.
3. Et Madonna, elle est belle, n'est-ce pas?
4. Ah non, elle n'est pas belle!

Pour utiliser chaque expression avec chaque dessin, changez les mots en italique.

A *Elle* est *forte* et *grande.*
   C'est *Madame Leclerc.*

B *Elle* est *élégante, Mademoiselle Colbert*?
   Oui, *elle* est très *élégante.*

C *Monsieur Dumas* est *beau,* n'est-ce pas?
   Non, *il* n'est pas *beau.*

1 forte, grande
2 grand, fort 
3 sévère, moche 
4 petite, élégante 
5 belle, folle 
6 beau, chouette 

Regardez maintenant: les fiches B1 et B2

Unité quatre — trente et un

Parlons

Série Deux

1. Tu aimes l'histoire?
2. J'aime bien l'histoire, mais je n'aime pas le français.
3. Moi, j'adore le français, mais je déteste l'éducation physique.

Pour utiliser chaque expression avec chaque dessin, changez les mots en italique.

A Tu aimes *l'éducation physique*?

Oui, j'aime (bien) *l'éducation physique*.

B Et *la chanson*?

J'adore *la chanson*.

C Tu aimes bien *Monsieur Ravel*?

Non, je n'aime pas *Monsieur Ravel*.

D Et *Toutou*?

Moi, je déteste *Toutou*.

Regardez maintenant: les fiches C1, C2 et C3

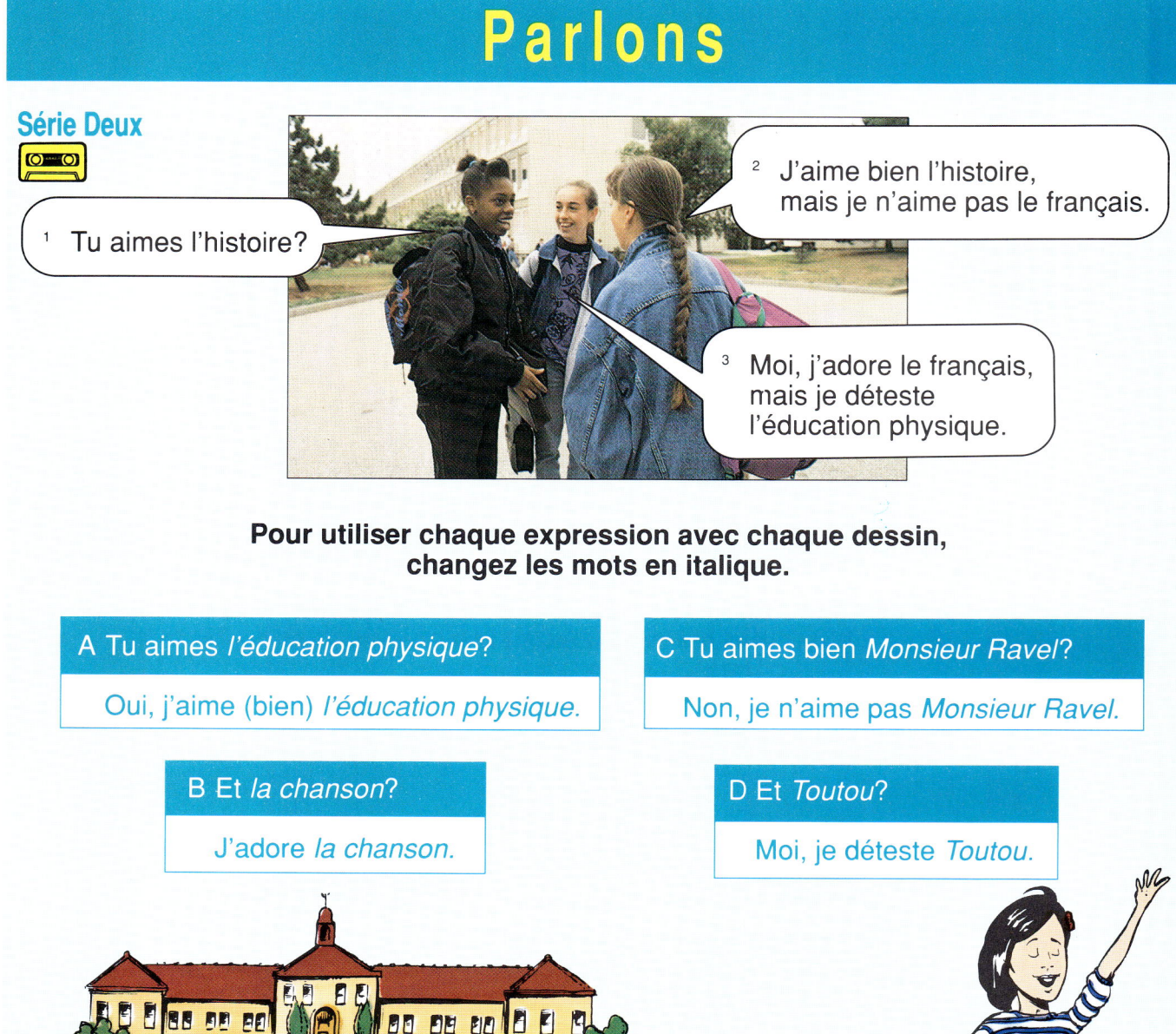

32 trente-deux

Unité quatre

Parlons

Série Trois

1. Il s'appelle comment, monsieur Laval?
2. Il s'appelle Michel.
3. Et il a quel âge?
4. Il a trente-trois ans, je crois.

17	dix-sept
18	dix-huit
19	dix-neuf
20	vingt
21	vingt et un
22	vingt-deux
23	vingt-trois
24	vingt-quatre
25	vingt-cinq
26	vingt-six
27	vingt-sept
28	vingt-huit
29	vingt-neuf
30	trente
31	trente et un
32	trente-deux

Pour utiliser chaque expression avec chaque dessin, changez les mots en italique.

Nom: Colbert (Mlle)
Prénom: Nadine
Âge: 29 ans
Matière: Le français

Nom: Leclerc (Mme)
Prénom: Sylvie
Âge: 24 ans
Matière: L'éducation physique

Nom: Ravel
Prénom: Maurice
Âge: 25 ans
Matière: La musique

Nom: Pappas (Mlle)
Prénom: Nicole
Âge: 29 ans
Matière: L'histoire

Nom: Baron
Prénom: François
Âge: 37 ans
Matière: L'anglais

A Il s'appelle comment, *Monsieur Baron*?
Il s'appelle *François*.

B Elle a quel âge, *Madame Leclerc*?
Elle a *vingt-quatre* ans, je crois.

C Qui est le professeur de *musique*?
Le professeur de *musique*, c'est Monsieur *Ravel*.

Regardez maintenant: les fiches D1, D2 et D3

Unité quatre

Parlons... avec un(e) partenaire

A: J'adore / J'aime | l'école. | Et toi?

*Moi, je suis **A**. Toi, tu es **B**.*

D'accord.

B: Moi? | Je n'aime pas / Je déteste | ça. | L'école est | moche. / folle.

A: Voilà | Monsieur Simon, Madame Leclerc, Monsieur Dumas, Mademoiselle Colbert, Monsieur Ravel, | le / la | directeur / prof | de l'école. / d'éducation physique. / de français. / de musique. / de géographie.

Il / Elle | est | chouette. / belle/beau. / sympa.

B: Il / Elle | n'est pas | chouette. / beau/belle. / sympa. | Il / Elle | est | sévère. / moche. / folle/fou.

L'école, c'est pour les fous.

A: Jules Verne, c'est une | bonne / belle | école.

B: L'école est | moche. / folle.

A: L'école est mon amour.

B: L'école est pour les fous.

A: Quel casse-pieds!

Regardez maintenant: les fiches E1 et E2

34 trente-quatre   Unité quatre

Parlons... en situation

LE PARTENAIRE IDÉAL

Somewhere in your class there is a perfect friend for you. This activity will help you find out who it is.

Firstly, choose from the list of adjectives below the five qualities you would want this perfect partner to have. Write them on a piece of paper.

grand(e)	riche
petite(e)	calme
intelligent(e)	honnête
marrant(e)	chouette
élégant(e)	sympa

Now you can start asking round the class, **Tu es intelligent(e)? Tu es riche?**

The answer will be, **Oui, je suis...** or
Non, je ne suis pas...

Make sure that you vary the pronunciation of the adjectives in the left-hand column according to whether you're speaking to a boy or a girl.

When you get five **Oui** answers, **c'est le partenaire idéal!**

SONDAGE SUR LES MATIÈRES

This is a survey to find out which are the most popular school subjects.

Make a list of the subjects you are doing this year (you don't have to include all of them) and then start asking people,

Tu aimes le français? etc.

The answers can be   **J'adore...**   10 points
J'aime...   7 points
Je n'aime pas...   2 points

After you have asked enough people you can count up the points for each subject.

Why not ask the maths teacher to show you how to put your results on a graph.

Regardez maintenant: la fiche F1

Ça c'est le français

1 DESCRIBING PEOPLE

In the last chapter you learned some very useful French adjectives and learned that they had one form for females (the feminine form) and another for males (the masculine form).

e.g. **Mademoiselle Colbert est élégante.**
Monsieur Dumas est élégant.

In fact, all French noun words are either masculine or feminine. So when you want to describe a thing, you have to make sure that the adjective matches it in gender, just as you would if you were talking about a person.

e.g. **un nom marrant**
a funny name
une chanson marrante
a funny song

In some cases, the difference between masculine and feminine is more obvious:

feminine	masculine
belle	beau
folle	fou

So, for most adjectives there is a difference in sound and spelling between the masculine and feminine forms. But there are some which have the same form for both genders.

e.g. **Mademoiselle Pappas est sévère.**
Monsieur Baron est sévère.

Others like **sévère** include:
**chouette   sympa   formidable   moche
calme   riche   honnête**

Study this table:

je suis riche	I am rich
tu es riche	you are rich
il est riche	he is rich
elle est riche	she is rich

2 EXPRESSING LIKES AND DISLIKES

You can ask a person if he or she likes something by saying,
Tu aimes...?

If someone asks you this question, you can answer,

Oui, j'aime...	Yes, I like...
J'adore	I love (adore)...
Non, je n'aime pas	No, I don't like...
Je déteste...	I hate (detest)...

Careful! if you say **J'aime** about people, you're saying you love them. If you just like them, say **J'aime bien.**

3 ASKING QUESTIONS

Tu aimes le français? Do you like French? This is the simplest way of asking a question in French: just use exactly the same words as you would for a statement and add a question mark.

If you are speaking, you have to put the question mark into the tone of your voice. You have to make it sound like a question.

4 N'EST-CE PAS?

Use this expression to check with someone to see if they agree with you.

e.g. **Tu aimes le français, n'est-ce pas?**
You like French, don't you?
Monsieur Dumas est chouette, n'est-ce pas?
Monsieur Dumas is great, isn't he?

5 NEGATIVES

To make a sentence negative in French, you use **ne...pas**

e.g. **Je ne suis pas grand.** I am not tall.

Often **ne** comes in front of a word beginning with a vowel and changes to **n'**.

e.g. **Elle n'est pas belle.**
She isn't beautiful.
Je n'aime pas le rock.
I don't like rock music.

Regardez maintenant: les fiches G1 et G2

L'Europe et la France

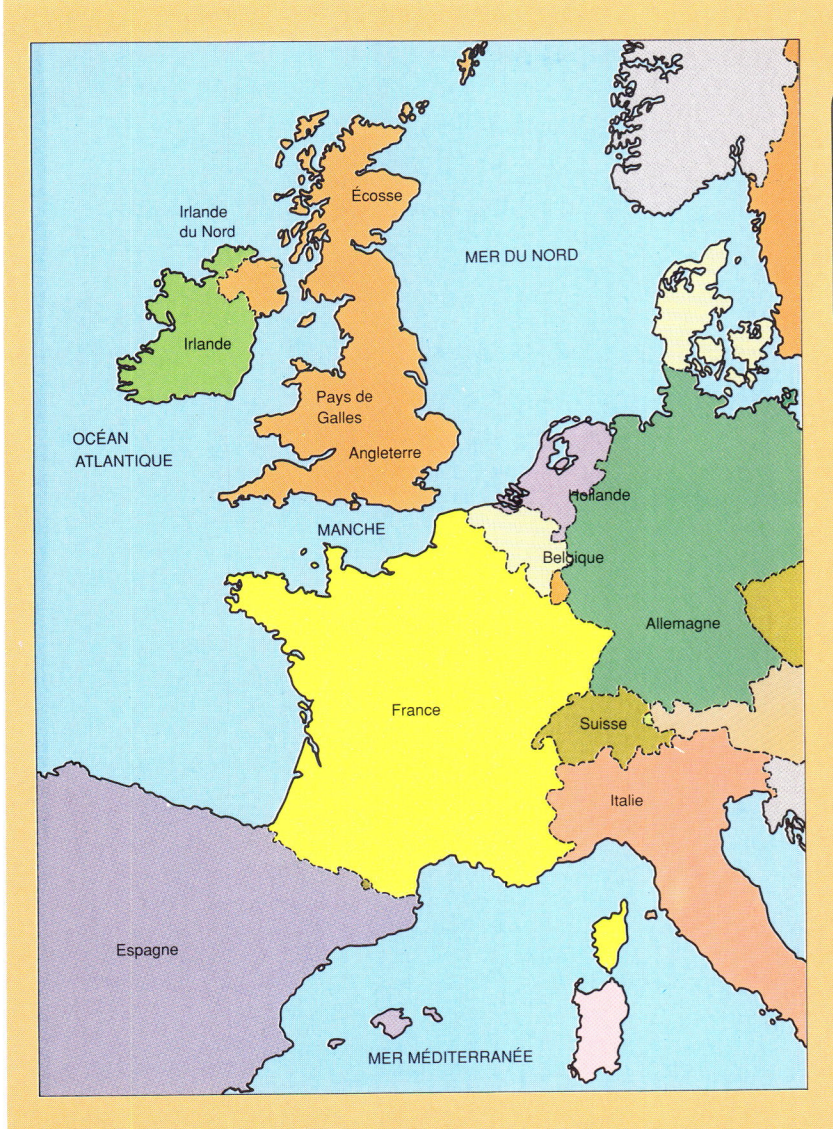

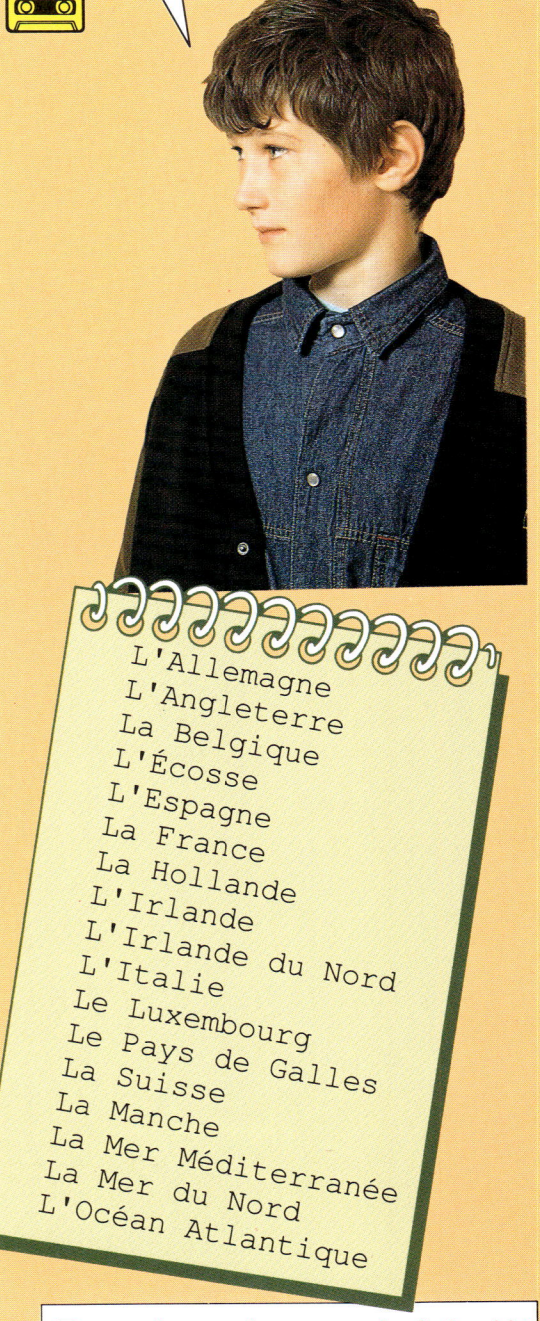

O-C-É-A-N A-T-L-A-N-T-I-Q-U-E
M-E-R D-U N-O-R-D
L-A M-A-N-C-H-E
É-C-O-S-S-E
P-A-Y-S D-E G-A-L-L-E-S
B-E-L-G-I-Q-U-E
F-R-A-N-C-E

L'Allemagne
L'Angleterre
La Belgique
L'Écosse
L'Espagne
La France
La Hollande
L'Irlande
L'Irlande du Nord
L'Italie
Le Luxembourg
Le Pays de Galles
La Suisse
La Manche
La Mer Méditerranée
La Mer du Nord
L'Océan Atlantique

We all know that although **les Îles Britanniques** - the British Isles - form part of **l'Europe**, they are separated from the mainland by sea. To travel from Britain to another country, you have to cross the sea - or use the Channel Tunnel.

If you live "on the continent" - in France or Belgium, for example - you can travel by car or train through more than 25 countries, each with its own language and own way of life.

Imagine a trip from Brussels to Rome! Starting in **la Belgique**, you might drive through **l'Allemagne** (Germany), **la France**, and **la Suisse** (Switzerland) before crossing **les Alpes** into **l'Italie**. Think of the different languages you would have to cope with.

Regardez maintenant: la fiche H1

Unité quatre   trente-sept   37

Les vacances en Grande-Bretagne

Lots of people from other countries come to **la Grande-Bretagne** on holiday. Here are two advertising brochures designed to attract French-speaking tourists to Great Britain. You'll be amazed at how much you'll understand!

hôtel ibis

Pour votre visite à Londres

**3 SUPER EMPLACEMENTS
3 SUPER HOTELS**

1. EUSTON – Au coeur de Londres
2. GREENWICH – Pour la Tamise et l'histoire
3. HEATHROW – Au départ des vols internationaux

Réservation gratuite par la réception de l'hôtel ou par RÉSINTER (Voir le Guide Ibis)

Printed in the UK

① Which river do you think **la Tamise** is?

② Why is it handy to stay at the Heathrow Ibis?

③ Make a list of six other words which are the same or nearly the same as in English.

④ Which three countries can you visit with Air Europe?

⑤ Besides reserving the day before your departure, how else can you reserve your flight?

⑥ What are the French words for c<u>ar</u> and p<u>lane</u>?

⑦ How many English words or phrases can you find on the second advertisement?

L'ANGLETERRE, L'ECOSSE, LE PAYS DE GALLES...
AVION + VOITURE   *air europe*

A PARTIR DE
1 090 F*
par pers./base 4 pers.

Paris Charles de Gaulle/London Gatwick.
Vous réservez à l'avance... ou la veille de votre départ... No problem !
Votre voiture ?
Prenez-la à l'aéroport ou au centre de Londres.
Up to you !

Fiesta Popular Plus

UN HOTEL,
UN BED & BREAKFAST,
UN APPARTEMENT,
UN COTTAGE...
CHOISISSEZ
AU FIL DE LA BROCHURE

Regardez maintenant: la fiche I1

38 trente-huit Unité quatre

Learning about language

LEARNING THE WORDS

One of your most important jobs as a language student is to build up a good store of vocabulary. There is no way out of it: at some point you have to make a personal effort to learn the French words that are used in each unit. Don't rely on the "sponge" method, hoping to soak up the new vocabulary simply by being there and participating in classroom activities.

So, how do you learn new vocabulary? Students often complain that they learn the words one day and forget them the next. Here are a few handy hints to help you memorise new words - after all, they are the bricks you need to build up your knowledge of the language.

1 For every single word you are studying, make up a personal system for remembering it. Often a word or sound association will help you. For example, how can you remember that **moche** means awful, horrible, yucky etc.?
   Well, say it a few times with a snarl and a sneer and think of mush or muck - and that's one word you've learned for life. The sillier your private memory method is, the more likely you are to remember the word.

2 Don't be satisfied with just running your eye up and down the word list a couple of times. Get busy with a pen and paper, write the words and pay attention to spelling them properly. Test yourself by covering first one language, then the other. Get Dad to "hear" you while he's cooking the dinner.

3 Divide and conquer! Don't try to learn too many words at one attempt. Divide the list into groups of a dozen or so words or expressions and tackle one section at a time. You will notice that the vocabulary pages in this book are divided into convenient sections.

4 Look for patterns in the language that will help you remember words and make good guesses when you can't remember. What is the French for classical and physical? What is the word for music? Bet you can't guess the French word for picnic!

Remember, it's up to you. You'll find a system that works for you. Why not have a discussion in class and see what ideas people come up with.

Leçon • **Les sons** • *Leçon* • **Les sons** • *Leçon*

When you are pronouncing the French **é** you have to produce a short sharp sound that is much shorter than the (southern) English ay sound. First say this in your best southern English accent to get that ay sound out of your system!

Hey, Ray, want to play today?

Now use your best French accent to practise these expressions.

Désirée est désolée.
Il est méchant.
Elle est élégante.
Je déteste la télé.

Unité quatre

Vocabulaire

C'EST BIEN LE MOT!

l'amour	love
bienvenue	welcome
la chanson	song
de, d'	of
l'école	school
la matière	subject
la musique classique	classical music
le nom	surname
pour	for
le prénom	given name
le/la professeur	teacher
le rock	rock music
toujours	always
un, une	a, an, one
voici	here is, here are

ADJECTIFS

belle, beau	beautiful
bonne, bon	good
calme	calm
chouette	great, cute
folle, fou	mad, crazy
formidable	fantastic, great
fort(e)	strong
honnête	honest
moche	ugly, awful, horrible
nouvelle, nouveau	new
sévère	strict
super	fantastic, terrific
sympa	nice, friendly

MATIÈRES

l'anglais	English
le dessin	art
l'éducation physique	physical education
le français	French
la géographie	geography
l'histoire	history
la musique	music
les maths	mathematics
les sciences	science

EXPRESSION UTILES

je crois	I think
ça suffit	that's enough
il a vingt-deux ans	he is twenty-two years old
le, la chouchou (du professeur)	teacher's pet
quel casse-pieds!	what a pain! what a bore!
s'il vous plaît	please
silence!	be quiet!
tous ensemble	all together
zut!	bother!
levez-vous!	stand up!
asseyez-vous	sit down!

Quel progrès!

Now you can do all these things in French!

- give more detailed descriptions of people
- agree and disagree about people and school
- express likes and dislikes about people or school
- give information about yourself
- ask for information about other people

Regardez maintenant: les fiches J1, J2, et J3

40 quarante

Unité quatre

UNITÉ CINQ
Bobot a tout

1. Doucement! Doucement, s'il vous plaît.
Venez ici. Regardez! Il y a des places ici.
Paul, ferme la porte. Sandrine, ouvre la fenêtre.

2. Bonjour, tout le monde.
Bonjour, Mademoiselle Colbert.

3. Ouvrez votre livre de français, s'il vous plaît. Non, Gilles, ça c'est le cahier. Ferme le cahier et ouvre le livre.
Excusez-moi, mademoiselle. Je n'ai pas de livre, aujourd'hui.
Ah bon?! Travaille avec Paul, alors.

4. Et maintenant, regardez la photo à la page dix-huit. Alors, ça, qu'est-ce que c'est?
C'est la lettre A, mademoiselle!

5. Silence! Taisez-vous!

6. Non, Gilles, c'est la Tour...la Tour...
...de France, mademoiselle?
Mais non, c'est la Tour Eiffel.

Unité cinq　　　　　　　　　　　　　quarante et un　41

7. Entrez!

8. Excusez-moi, mademoiselle, Monsieur Ravel et moi...
— Elle est en retard.

9. Oui, mais c'est le chouchou de Monsieur Ravel.

10. Ça suffit, maintenant. Assieds-toi. Bravo, Nathalie. C'est une belle chanson, *J'adore l'école*.
— Merci beaucoup, mademoiselle.
— Et maintenant ouvrez votre cahier.

11. Mademoiselle, mademoiselle. Regardez Roger. Il n'a pas de cahier, il n'a pas de livre...

12. Roger! Pas de livre? Pas de stylo? Pas de crayon...?
— Mais, mademoiselle, j'ai tout ici dans l'ordinateur... Il s'appelle Robobot.
— TAIS-TOI, NATHALIE!

42 quarante-deux Unité cinq

13. — Mais Roger, c'est impossible.
— Oui, Roger, tu es impossible.

14. — Mais mademoiselle, regardez! Voilà le livre. Voilà le cahier. Bobot a tout.
— Pas tout! Où est le surligneur?

15. — Voici le surligneur... et voici le Scotch.

16. — Ça alors, c'est chouette!

18. — Bravo, la classe! Et maintenant, travaillez en silence!

Regardez maintenant: les fiches A1, A2 et A3.

Unité cinq — quarante-trois — 43

Parlons

Série Un

1. Qu'est-ce que c'est?
2. C'est un cartable.
3. Et ça, c'est un surligneur, n'est-ce pas?
4. Non, ce n'est pas un surligneur, c'est une trousse.

1 un cartable
2 un crayon
3 un livre
4 un cahier
5 une trousse
6 un stylo
7 une gomme
8 un surligneur
9 une règle

Pour utiliser chaque expression avec chaque dessin, changez les mots en italique.

A Ça, qu'est-ce que c'est en français?

Ça, c'est *un cahier*.

B Où est *le livre*?

Voilà *le livre*.
   ou
Je n'ai pas de *livre* aujourd'hui.

C Ça, c'est *un stylo*, n'est-ce pas?

Non, ce n'est pas un *stylo*, c'est *un surligneur*.

D Tu as *un crayon rouge*?

Oui, voilà.
   ou
Non, je n'ai pas de *crayon rouge*.

Regardez maintenant: les fiches B1 et B2

44 quarante-quatre   Unité cinq

Parlons

Série Deux

1. Levez-vous, s'il vous plaît.
2. Mais...Charles, lève-toi.

Pour utiliser chaque expression avec chaque dessin, changez les mots en italique.

A *Regardez la fenêtre*!

   Regardez la fenêtre, s'il vous plaît.

B *Asseyez-vous*!

   Paul! *Assieds-toi*!

Regardez maintenant: les fiches C1 et C2

Unité cinq

Parlons

Série Trois

1. Tu as beaucoup de poissons.
2. Oui, j'ai le rouge, [etc.]
3. Où est le poisson jaune?
4. Voilà le poisson jaune.

bleu — rouge — violet — vert — rose — brun — jaune — blanc — noir — orange — gris

Pour utiliser chaque expression avec chaque dessin, changez les mots en italique.

A Où est le poisson *noir*?	B Tu aimes le *rouge*?
Voilà le poisson *noir*.	Non, je n'aime pas le *rouge*.

C Et le *vert*?

J'adore le *vert*.
Je déteste le *vert*.

Regardez maintenant:
les fiches D1 et D2

46 quarante-six

Unité cinq

Parlons... avec un(e) partenaire

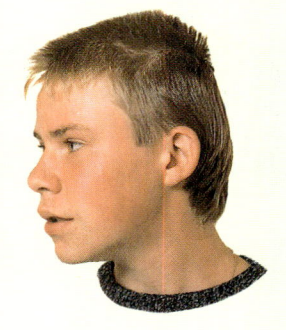

*Moi, je suis **A**. Toi, tu es **B**.*

D'accord.

A | Bonjour, | monsieur. / mademoiselle. / madame.

B | Bonjour.

A | Un stylo / Une trousse / Un surligneur | rouge, / vert(e), / noir(e), | s'il vous plaît.

B | Excusez-moi. / Je suis désolé(e). | Je n'ai pas de | stylo / trousse / surligneur | rouge. / vert(e). / noir(e).

A | Ah non! / Ça alors! | C'est impossible! / Quelle catastrophe! | Pas de | stylo?! / trousse?! / surligneur?!

B | Pas de | stylo! / trousse! / surligneur! | Pas de | cahier! / cartable! / livre! | Pas de | gomme! / règle! / crayon! | Je suis désolé(e).

A | Et ça, qu'est-ce que c'est?

B | C'est un ordinateur. Il s'appelle | Bobot. / Paritel. / Claude.

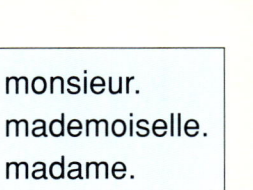

A | C'est | fantastique! / chouette! / super! | Avec un ordinateur, j'ai tout. Merci, | monsieur. / mademoiselle. / madame.

B | Au revoir. / À bientôt.

Unité cinq   quarante-sept   47

Parlons... en situation

LIBRAIRIE-PAPETERIE

In France, most schools now provide textbooks, although pupils have to pay a fine if they lose or damage them. However, pupils often have to buy their own stationery items at **une Librairie-Papeterie** - a shop which sells books and stationery.

Imagine that your parents are working in France for a year and that you are going to go to school there. You have to start in a few days, so you go to the local stationers' to buy what you need. First of all, you may need to ask the French name for some of the items you need. Then you have to ask the shop assistant where each item is. Sometimes they can show you, but in some cases they have sold out.

You might want to ask how much things cost. If so, here's how to do it.

C'est combien? — How much is it?
Ça, c'est seize francs. — That's 16 francs.

You might also want to say:
C'est tout? — Is that all?

Before you begin this activity, spend some time setting up a stationers' shop in your classroom. Make a sign for the shop saying **Librairie - Papeterie.**

À L'ÉCOLE

Now imagine that you are collecting the textbooks that you need for the year ahead. As you collect the different textbooks you tell the teacher what you think about different subjects. (You can use **j'aime, je déteste** etc.)

OBEDIENCE SCHOOL

You have just opened the **Vie de chien** obedience school for dogs. Most of the dogs are coming along nicely, but Gilles' and Roger's dogs, Toutou and Bach, often need individual attention. Désirée's dog, Offenbach, just won't stop yapping.

See if you can train the dogs to sit, come here, look here, be quiet, open and close the door. Treat them as a group and test some of them individually.

If you volunteer to be one of the dogs, your job is to show that you can understand the commands.

(Psst! If you're not sure which command to use when, look at page 52.)

Viens ici, Auguste!

Ouah! Ouah!

Regardez maintenant: les fiches E1 et E2

Ça c'est le français

1 CLASSROOM COMMANDS

You'll notice that the same classroom command can sound a bit different, depending on whether it's given to the class as a whole or to an individual member of the class. If you look at the table below, you'll notice that they are written differently too.

whole group	individual
ouvrez le livre **fermez la fenêtre** **regardez la photo** **travaillez en silence**	**ouvre le livre** **ferme la fenêtre** **regarde la photo** **travaille en silence**

What about **venez** and **viens**?

Stop being difficult.

Some commands follow a different pattern.

whole group	individual
levez-vous **asseyez-vous** **taisez-vous**	**lève-toi** **assieds-toi** **tais-toi**

2 HOW TO SAY "A" AND "THE"

You may already have noticed that the words you use for a and the depend on whether the words you are using them with are masculine or feminine.

	the	a
feminine	**la**	**une**
masculine	**le**	**un**

e.g. **la fenêtre**   **le crayon**
     une trousse **un cahier**

As you are learning new words in French, learn them with the correct word for the. Sometimes it is hard to remember which gender (masculine or feminine) a word is. Even experienced students can find it difficult - and sometimes, even French people! So keep trying and don't be discouraged.

You have to make a special effort to remember the gender of words beginning with a vowel.

e.g. **l'école (f)**   **l'ordinateur (m)**

In these cases it may be better to learn **une école, un ordinateur.**

3 HOW TO SAY "A" WITH NEGATIVES

Je n'ai pas de livre aujourd'hui.
I haven't got a book today.

Notice that in French you don't use the normal word for a (**un, une**) after **pas**. You use **de** instead.

4 WHAT A...

Quelle classe fantastique!
What a fantastic class!

When you feel strongly about something and you want to let people know, you can use **quel** with a masculine word or **quelle** with a feminine word.

e.g. **Quelle catastrophe!**   What a disaster!

    Quel ordinateur!   What a computer!

Regardez maintenant: les fiches F1 et F2

quarante-neuf   Unité cinq

L'Hexagone

This map has some of the main cities in France marked on it. Use a ruler and the scale given for the map to get a rough idea of the distances between the following cities.

1. Paris - Strasbourg
2. Lyon - Paris
3. Toulouse - Bordeaux
4. Paris - Marseille
5. Nice - Lille

If you stick to the **autoroutes** and average 100 kilometres (70 miles) per hour in your Citroën, Renault or Peugeot, how long will these trips take you?

Can you think of trips of similar distances between cities in Britain? For example, going from Paris to Lyon would be like travelling from London to Glasgow or from Plymouth to Newcastle.

One good way to remember where French cities (and mountains and rivers) are situated is to practise drawing quick maps of France. This is easy when you realise that the country is shaped roughly like a hexagon - a six-sided shape. In fact, the French sometimes call their country **l'Hexagone**. You'll become expert at producing rough maps of France and marking various geographical details as you learn about them.

1 centimètre égale 100 kilomètres

Regardez maintenant: la fiche G1

Sur le pont d'Avignon

50 cinquante

Unité cinq

L'École en France

How would you like to go to school in France? There are some advantages, you know. For example, you can have every Wednesday off school (Wednesday afternoon when you're older), and we'll give you two hours for lunch every day. Don't worry about a uniform; pupils at French schools don't wear them. And you'd enjoy the two and a half months of summer holiday break from June to September. Sounds great, doesn't it?

Perhaps you should also know that on most days school starts at 8.00 a.m. and goes through until 5.00 p.m. And then there are a couple of hours of classes on Saturday mornings. And you can only expect a short break over the Christmas period.

French pupils have to take their studies very seriously. They all follow the same national curriculum and are expected to reach a high standard. Exams are an important part of school life in France. If you fail, you must repeat the year - no excuses, no arguments! Still interested in joining?

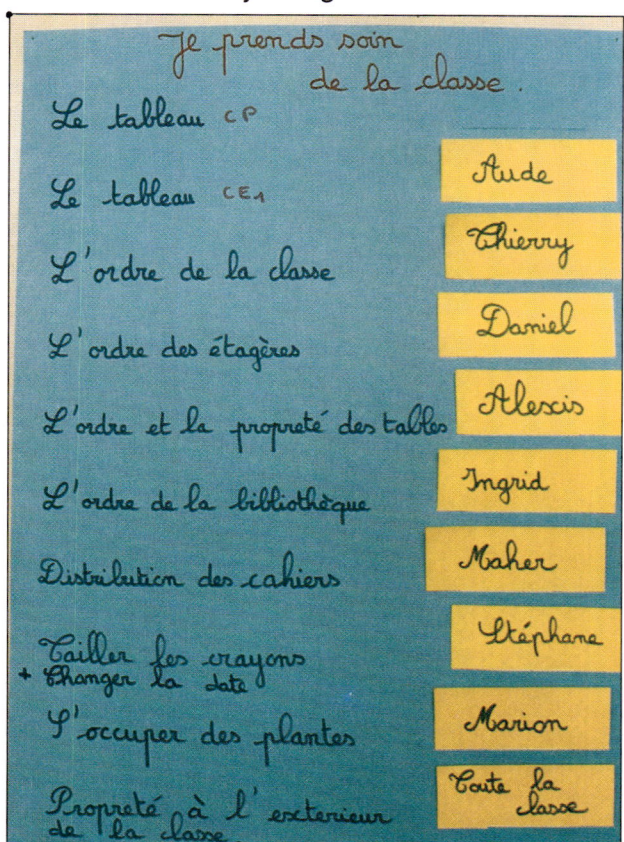

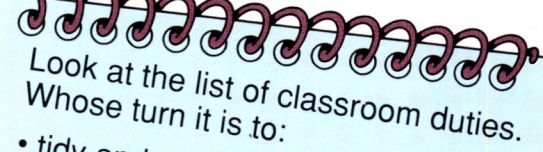

J'ai tout ici dans l'ordinateur

Look at the list of classroom duties. Whose turn it is to:
- tidy and clean the tables?
- give out the exercise books?
- sharpen the pencils?
- look after the plants?
- clean outside the classroom?
- tidy the classroom?

Regardez maintenant: la fiche H1

Unité cinq

Vocabulaire

C'EST BIEN LE MOT!

alors	well, then
aujourd'hui	today
avec	with
ça	that
fantastique	fantastic
la fenêtre	window
ici	here
la librairie	bookshop
la papeterie	newsagents', stationers'
la place	seat
la porte	door
tout	all, everything
votre	your

EXPRESSIONS UTILES

à la page 17	on page 17
beaucoup de	lots of
c'est combien?	how much is it?
c'est impossible!	it's impossible!
doucement!	quietly! slowly!
en retard	late
en silence	in silence
entrez!	come in!
il y a	there is, there are
où est...?	where is...?
qu'est-ce que c'est?	what is it?
tout le monde	everybody

À L'ÉCOLE

le cahier	exercise book
le crayon	pencil
la gomme	rubber
le livre	book
l'ordinateur (m)	computer
la règle	ruler
le cartable	(school) bag
le stylo	pen
le surligneur	highlighter
la trousse	pencil case

LES COULEURS

rouge	red
violet	mauve
bleu	blue
rose	pink
vert	green
noir	black
brun	brown
jaune	yellow
blanc	white
orange	orange
gris	grey

LES MOTS D'ORDRE EN CLASSE

AU SINGULIER	AU PLURIEL	
Assieds-toi!	**Asseyez-vous!**	Sit down!
Lève-toi!	**Levez-vous!**	Stand up!
Viens ici!	**Venez ici!**	Come here!
Regarde ici!	**Regardez ici!**	Look this way!
Tais-toi!	**Taisez-vous!**	Be quiet!
Ouvre la porte!	**Ouvrez la porte!**	Open the door!
Ferme la porte!	**Fermez la porte!**	Shut the door!

C'est le cartable de Stéphane!

Mais non, regarde!

Ah, je suis désolé; le cartable de Stéphane est bleu.

Regardez maintenant: les fiches l1 et l2

52 cinquante-deux

Unité cinq

Leçon • Les sons • Leçon • Les sons • Leçon

The French **ou** sound requires a special effort from people used to speaking with a British accent. We have already seen that the **u** sound is thin and piercing. The **ou** sound is a deep, dark sound for which you must push your lips well forward.

Practise in front of the mirror!

Practise contrasting the **u** and **ou** sounds in the following sentences.

Ça suffit, Toutou!
Où est Luc?
Ouvre la trousse, Julie!
Quel âge as-tu, Louis?

Ou!!

Quel progrès!

Bravo! Now you can use your French to do all these things:

- ask what something is
- say what something is
- ask where someone or something is
- say where someone or something close to you is
- correct someone when they're wrong
- tell people to do things
- ask for things in a shop
- ask how much something costs
- say how much something costs

- oh yes, and train dogs!

Viens ici, Minette.

Je regrette, je suis en retard.

Regardez maintenant: les fiches J1 et J2

cinquante-trois 53

UNITÉ SIX
Bon week-end!

1. — C'est le week-end! Formidable!! Qu'est-ce que tu vas faire pendant le week-end, Nathalie?
— Je vais chanter et danser pendant tout le week-end. Samedi matin, j'ai une classe de danse et dimanche après-midi, j'ai une répétition pour *Les Misérables*...

2. — *Les Misérables*? Qu'est-ce que c'est?
— C'est une comédie musicale. Pour moi, le théâtre, c'est la vie! Et toi, qu'est-ce que tu vas faire?

3. — Pas grand-chose. Demain, je vais regarder la télé et écouter de la musique, et dimanche, je vais aider maman. Elle va faire le ménage. Quelle barbe!!

4. — Dis donc, Gilles, qu'est-ce que tu vas faire demain?
— Pas grand-chose. Je vais peut-être faire mes devoirs. Après ça, je vais nager, à la piscine.

5. — Et toi, Paul?
— Pas grand-chose. Je vais jouer au tennis, je crois. Moi, je suis un grand joueur.
— *C'est un grand menteur aussi.*

6. — Venez chez moi, alors. J'ai un terrain de tennis, une piscine, une salle de jeux.
— D'accord. Où est-ce que tu habites?

54 cinquante-quatre — Unité six

J'habite rue Vermont, numéro dix-sept à vingt et un. Est-ce que tu as un chauffeur, Paul?
Moi? Euh, oui, mais il est en vacances.
Ah bon? Alors Frédéric va passer chez toi et puis chez Gilles. À demain.
7
D'accord. À demain chez toi.
Menteur. Tu n'as pas de chauffeur.
NM-76
8
Samedi après-midi. La maison de Roger est très grande.
Quelle maison énorme!
9
Debussy, tu ne manges pas beaucoup. Pourquoi? Tu n'aimes pas le poisson aujourd'hui?
Mais, oui, bien sûr! Debussy, c'est un chat extraordinaire.
Est-ce que le chat mange toujours à table?
10
Pourquoi est-ce que je mange ici tout seul?
11
Oui, Debussy est vraiment extra. C'est un chat très rare. Il y a seulement dix-neuf chats comme Debussy dans le monde.
12
Tu as une très grande maison.
13

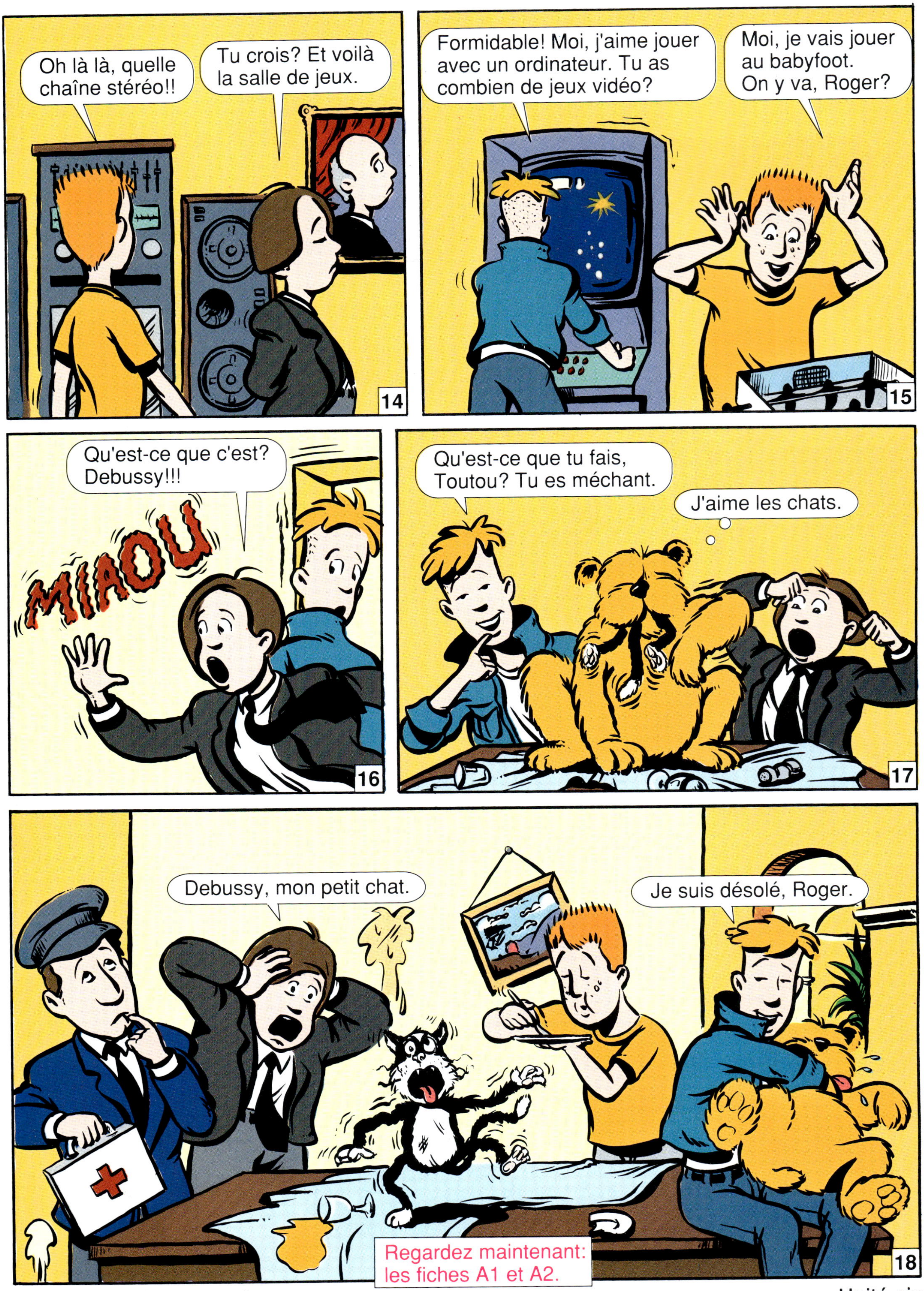

Regardez maintenant:
les fiches A1 et A2.

Parlons

Série Un

1. Qu'est-ce que tu vas faire pendant le week-end?
2. Samedi, je vais danser et dimanche, je vais aller à la piscine.
3. Et Catherine, qu'est-ce qu'elle va faire?
4. Elle va jouer au tennis.

Pour utiliser chaque expression avec chaque dessin, changez les mots en italique.

A Qu'est-ce que tu vas faire *samedi*, *Nathalie*?

Samedi, je vais danser.

samedi

dimanche

B Qu'est-ce que tu vas faire pendant le week-end, *Paul*?

Samedi, je vais jouer au tennis. Dimanche, je vais écouter de la musique.

C Et *Gilles*, qu'est-ce qu'*il* va faire?

Il va faire ses devoirs et nager à la piscine.

samedi

samedi

samedi

dimanche

dimanche

dimanche

dimanche

Regardez maintenant: les fiches B1, B2 et B3

Unité six

cinquante-sept 57

Parlons

Série Deux

1. Où est-ce que tu habites?
2. J'habite rue de la Gare, numéro 21D.
3. Est-ce que tu as une petite maison?
4. Non, j'ai un grand appartement.

Pour utiliser chaque expression avec chaque dessin, changez les mots en italique.

A Où est-ce que tu habites, *Roger*?

J'habite *rue Vermont*, numéro *17 à 21*.

B Et *Paul*, où est-ce qu'*il* habite?

Il habite *avenue de l'École*, numéro *28*.

C Est-ce que tu as *un terrain de tennis*, *Sandrine*?
ou
Est-ce que tu as *un chauffeur*, *Sandrine*?

Oui, j'ai *un terrain de tennis*.
ou
Non, je n'ai pas de *chauffeur*.

D Est-ce que *Gilles* a *une grande maison*?

Non, *il* a *une petite maison*.

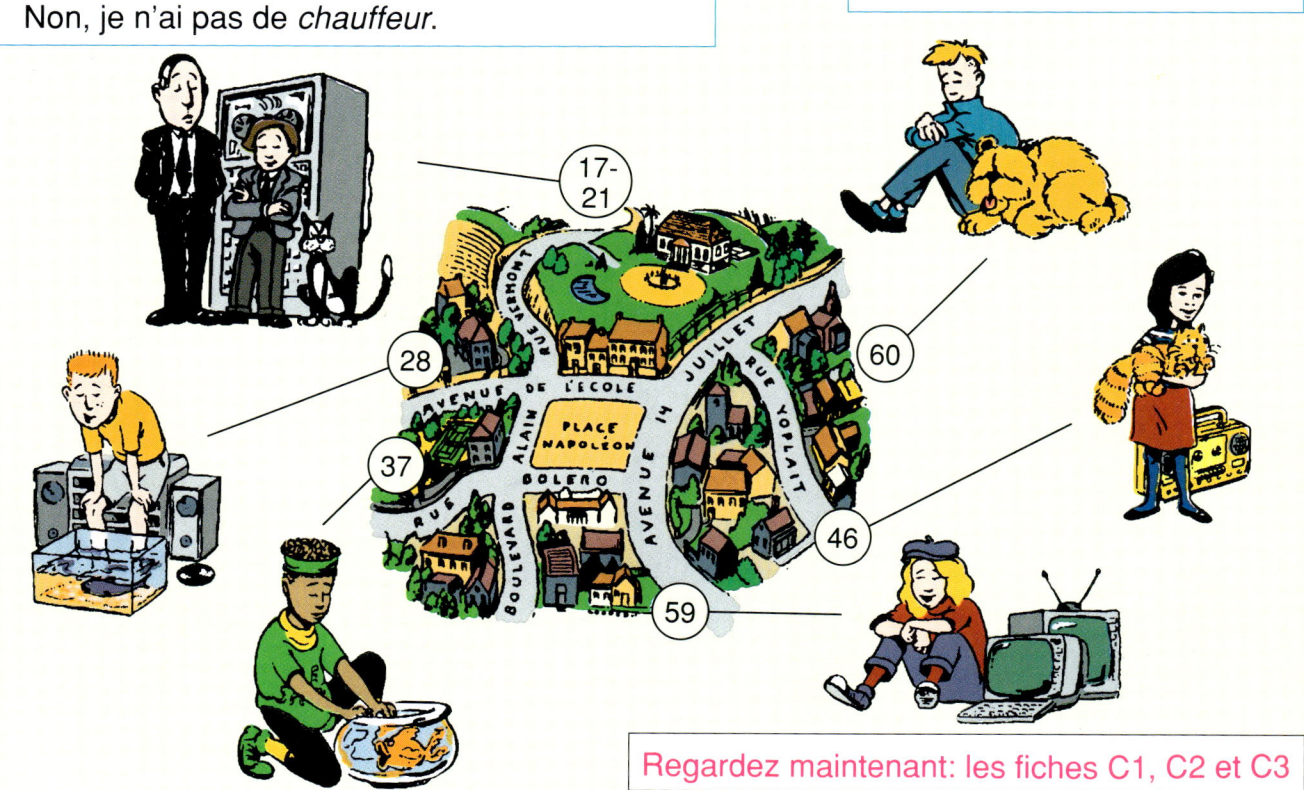

Regardez maintenant: les fiches C1, C2 et C3

58 cinquante-huit

Unité six

Parlons... avec un(e) partenaire

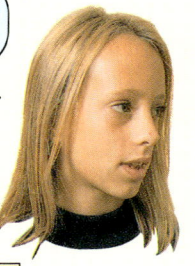

Moi, je suis **A**. Toi, tu es **B**.

D'accord.

| A | C'est vendredi | matin.
après-midi.
soir. | Formidable!
Fantastique!
Extra! |

| B | J'aime
J'adore | le week-end. Qu'est-ce que tu vas faire? |

| A | Vendredi soir,
Samedi matin,
Dimanche après-midi, | je vais | regarder la télé.
écouter de la musique.
faire mes devoirs.
aider maman. |

| B | Chouette!
Quelle barbe! | Moi, je vais jouer | au tennis.
au babyfoot.
avec mon ordinateur. |

| A | Viens chez moi, alors. J'ai | un terrain de tennis.
une salle de jeux.
un ordinateur extraordinaire. |

| B | Tu habites où?
Où est-ce que tu habites? |

| A | 76, rue Gambetta.
81, avenue Michelin.
98, boulevard Arpège. |

| B | D'accord. À | samedi matin,
samedi soir,
dimanche après-midi, | alors. |

| A | Au revoir. |

```
40 quarante
41 quarante et un
42 quarante-deux
50 cinquante
51 cinquante et un
52 cinquante-deux
60 soixante
61 soixante et un
62 soixante-deux
70 soixante-dix
71 soixante et onze
72 soixante-douze
Attention!
80 quatre-vingts
81 quatre-vingt-un
82 quatre-vingt-deux
90 quatre-vingt-dix
91 quatre-vingt-onze
92 quatre-vingt-douze
```

Moi, je vais jouer au babyfoot. Et toi?

Regardez maintenant: les fiches D1, D2 et D3

Unité six   cinquante-neuf   59

Parlons... en situation

1 EST-CE QUE TU AS ... CHEZ TOI?

Your task is to carry out a survey in your class to find out who has what at home.

Take a sample of about ten students. Your teacher will give you the survey sheet you need. You have to ask each of the students you interview if they have each of the items listed on the sheet.

e.g. **Est-ce que tu as un chat chez toi?**
Est-ce que tu as une piscine chez toi?

Oui, j'ai un chien chez moi.

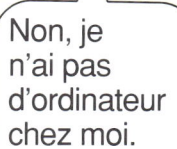

They will tell you whether they have that item.

e.g. **Oui, j'ai un chat chez moi.**
Non, je n'ai pas de piscine.

Be ready to report your results to the rest of the class. Say how many students and what percentage of the sample had each item.

e.g. **un chien - quatre personnes (quarante pour cent)**
un ordinateur - trois personnes (trente pour cent)

Non, je n'ai pas d'ordinateur chez moi.

2 VIENS CHEZ MOI.

It's after school on Friday afternoon, and you and a friend are talking about what you will do at the weekend. After you both come up with some ideas about what you might do - in French of course - you decide to go either to your friend's house or to your place. You have to decide when to go, to what address, and what you will do there.

J'habite 61, rue Tahure.

3 QU'EST-CE QUE TU AIMES FAIRE PENDANT LE WEEK-END?

Your task is to carry out a survey on weekend activities in your class, to find out which are the most popular and which are the most unpopular. Your teacher will give you the survey sheet you need. The two questions you have to ask are:

Qu'est-ce que tu aimes faire pendant le week-end?
Qu'est-ce que tu n'aimes pas faire pendant le week-end?

Take a sample of five students. Each one should be able to give you five likes and five dislikes.

Be ready to report your findings to the rest of the class.

Pendant le week-end j'aime aider maman!

Regardez maintenant: la fiche E1

Unité six

Ça c'est le français

1 TALKING ABOUT WHAT YOU ARE GOING TO DO

Je vais jouer au tennis et regarder la télé.
Qu'est-ce que **tu vas** faire?
Et Nathalie? Elle **va** chanter et danser pendant tout le week-end.

I'm going to play tennis and watch T.V.
What are you going to do?
And Nathalie? She's going to sing and dance all weekend.

2 TALKING ABOUT WHAT YOU LIKE DOING

J'aime aller au ciné.
Qu'est-ce que **tu aimes** faire?
Et Gilles? **Il aime** nager à la piscine.

I like to go to the cinema.
What do you like to do?
And Gilles? He likes swimming in the pool.

3 MORE ABOUT ASKING QUESTIONS

The simplest way of asking a question in French is to use a questioning tone of voice.

e.g. **Le chat mange toujours à table?**
Does the cat always eat at the table?

Another common way is to begin your question with **Est-ce que...**

e.g. **Est-ce que le chat mange toujours à table?**
Does the cat always eat at the table?

Est-ce que is used after **pourquoi** (why).

e.g. **Pourquoi est-ce que je mange ici tout seul?**
Why am I eating here all alone?

Est-ce que can also be used with **où** (where).

e.g. **Tu habites où?**
Where do you live?
Où est-ce que tu habites?
Where do you live?

* Don't let expressions like **Qu'est-ce que...?** and **Est-ce que...?** put you off because they look complicated. When you're speaking French, think of them as 'kesker' and 'esker'.

4 MORE ABOUT SAYING 'THE'

	singular	plural
masculine	**le**	**les**
feminine	**la**	**les**
feminine or masculine	**l'**	**les**

e.g. **le** chat   **les** chats
     la maison **les** maisons
     l'école   **les** écoles

5 THE PLURAL OF NOUNS

Most French nouns, like most English nouns, can be changed from singular to plural by adding **-s**.

e.g. chat   chat**s**
     école   école**s**

Some French nouns follow a different pattern.

e.g. jeu   jeu**x**

Note:
These changes from singular to plural only affect the way you write the words. They make no difference to the way you pronounce them.

> Pourquoi est-ce que je mange ici tout seul?

Regardez maintenant: les fiches F1 et F2.

Unité six — soixante et un 61

Quatre-vingt-seize heures à Paris

Félicitations! Your prize for winning the Unité Six vocabulary learning competition is a trip for two to Paris.

You arrive on Friday morning and stay until Tuesday morning - 96 hours in Paris!! It's hard to realise that this may well be about the amount of class time you will spend learning French this year. One long weekend! Makes you proud of how much you already know, doesn't it? Anyway, it's time to begin your visit to the French capital...

Look, your bus is waiting for you. I wonder why the tour is called **Paris à la carte**?

Get going and see how many of the sights you can see!

La cathédrale Notre-Dame, the cathedral of Our Lady, is on an island in the River Seine.

La cathédrale Notre-Dame est très belle et très grande.

If you make the long, winding climb to the roof of Notre-Dame, you can meet these gargoyles. They have a great view but they look forward to evenings when they can have some time off.

Qu'est-ce que tu vas faire samedi soir?

Je vais jouer au babyfoot, je crois.

This is part of what the gargoyles can see...**un bateau-mouche** on the Seine. You'll have to take one of these boat rides. It's a great way to see Paris.

Regarde! C'est Notre-Dame.

Mmm... J'adore les bateaux-mouches.

You can't go to Paris and not see **la Tour Eiffel.** Of course, young Parisians take it for granted. It has been their city's most famous landmark for a hundred years. They think the concrete areas near the tower are ideal places for **les patins à roulettes** (roller-skating) and **les planches à roulettes** (skateboarding).

La Tour Eiffel a 100 ans. Moi aussi!

One thing you can never complain about in Paris is the public transport. The underground railway system, called the **Métro**, is **fantastique, super, extra**! In the city of Paris you are never more than 500 metres from a **Métro** station.

Here's **l'église du Sacré-Cœur**, the church of the Sacred Heart. It dominates the city's highest hill. If you don't feel like climbing to the top now, why not join in and have a dance with **les marottes** here at the foot of the hill?

L'église du Sacré-Cœur est à Montmartre.

Well done! You have climbed the stairs to the top of **Montmartre** (or did you take the **funiculaire**?) and you have found the **Place du Tertre**, tucked away behind **Sacré-Cœur**. This little square is famous for the artists who paint there.

Unité six

Le Louvre is the largest art gallery and museum in France. (Leonardo da Vinci's painting of the Mona Lisa is just one of the thousands of paintings you can see there.) This new building at the Louvre has just been completed. It's made entirely of glass. Some people hate it, other love it!
Et toi, tu aimes ça?

L'Arc de Triomphe is another famous Parisian landmark. It dominates the most famous of all streets in Paris, **l'Avenue des Champs-Élysées**. It was Napoléon's idea to build this Triumphal Arch. Now there is an even bigger arch at the other end of the **Champs-Élysées**, **La Grande Arche de la Défense**, built by **Président Mitterand**.

L'Arc de Triomphe est grand...

...mais La Grande Arche de la Défense est énorme.

Regardez maintenant: les fiches G1 et G2

Huit raisons de visiter la Grande-Bretagne

Anglo Continental

Oui, parlons anglais! 15 jours de réels progrès dans la langue, tout en pratiquant le tennis, le squash, l'équitation, le golf, le bowling.

Les fameux "double decker bus".

L'Anglais en Angleterre

PAYS DE GALLES: VERT ET BEAU

Bed & Breakfast

200 familles vous attendent pour vivre complètement à l'anglaise. Pour 3 nuits ou plus, vous choisissez entre le Bed & Breakfast, la demi-pension ou la pension complète.

**3 NUITS + 3 BREAKFAST
525 F
par personne**

**UNE CHAUMIÈRE MÉDIÉVALE
7 NUITS À PARTIR DE
375 FRANCS**

LA VIE DE COTTAGE

Séjournez dans un de nos 800 cottages en Angleterre, en Écosse ou au Pays de Galles.

OUI, ON MANGE BIEN EN ANGLETERRE

OPEN TO VIEW

HERITAGE PASS

La carte "British Heritage" est valable 15 jours ou un mois. Cette carte vous ouvre les portes de 600 châteaux, musées, abbayes et jardins.

Le légendaire musée de Madame Tussaud, avec sa Chambre d'Horreurs.

Unité six   soixante-cinq   65

Petits poèmes

J'adore la musique
Rock ou classique
C'est fantastique!

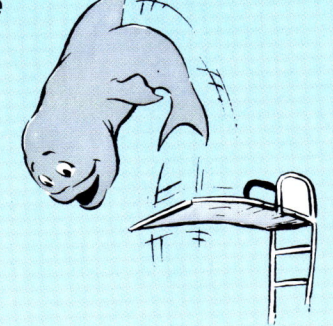

J'ai un petit poisson rouge
Il aime le français
Il adore **Ça bouge**.

Mon poisson s'appelle Justine
Elle aime nager dans la piscine
Mon oiseau s'appelle Christine
Elle aime chanter dans la cuisine.

You could do better than that?
All right then, try!!

...And here's a poem by a real poet!

Page d'écriture

*Deux et deux quatre
quatre et quatre huit
huit et huit font seize...
Répétez! dit le maître
Deux et deux quatre
quatre et quatre huit
huit et huit font seize.
Mais voilà l'oiseau-lyre
qui passe dans le ciel
l'enfant le voit
l'enfant l'entend
l'enfant l'appelle:
Sauve-moi
joue avec moi
oiseau!*

Jacques Prévert.

Two and two four
four and four eight
eight and eight make sixteen...
Repeat! says the teacher
Two and two four
four and four eight
eight and eight make sixteen...
But there's the lyrebird
passing by in the sky
the child sees it
the child hears it
the child calls to it:
Save me
Play with me
bird!

Regardez maintenant: la fiche H1

66 soixante-six   Unité six

Learning about language

POSITIVE READING SKILLS

Here are some useful do's and don'ts when reading in a foreign language.

DO
- Tackle the reading passage confidently.
- Concentrate on what you do know.
- Use all available clues (e.g. pictures, charts, maps) to help you make reasonable guesses at the meaning of a difficult section.
- Aim for an overall understanding of the passage - even if this means leaving a couple of small mysteries unsolved.

DON'T
- Be put off by words and expressions you haven't learned yet.
- Wait until you have looked up every word in a dictionary or vocabulary list before moving on to the next sentence.
- Tell yourself you can't understand unless every single word is crystal clear to you.

You know, you probably already have this commonsense attitude when you are reading in English. All of us, even the most intelligent, experienced readers, come across words we have never seen before. It is not often that we put down the book and go looking for a dictionary before continuing. What do you do?

Have a look at the French tourist advertisements about Great Britain on page 65.

- Look for English words that have been borrowed by French.
- Find the French words that are now also part of our language.
- Make a list of the French words that are so similar to English that you just couldn't go wrong.

The similarity between the two languages means that you always have a flying start when reading French. **200 familles vous attendent pour vivre complètement à l'anglaise.** This is probably the hardest sentence on the page. Start with what you know and see how much you can work out before you reach for a dictionary. Try similar tactics on some of the other lines.

Leçon • Les sons • Leçon • Les sons • Leçon

If you ever wondered what that dangly thing at the back of your throat was for, now you know: it's to help you pronounce the French **r** correctly!! If you really want to sound French you have to practise until you get it right. Use these English and French words to highlight the difference between the **r** sounds in each language.

Paris	**Paris**
Roger	**Roger**
director	**directeur**
grand	**grand**
terrain	**terrain**
regard	**regarde**

You will sound even more French if you pronounce the **r** at the end of words like these:

**faire
extraordinaire
pour
la Tour
chauffeur
menteur
au revoir
le soir**

Don't forget, practice makes perfect.

Unité six   soixante-sept

Bon week-end!

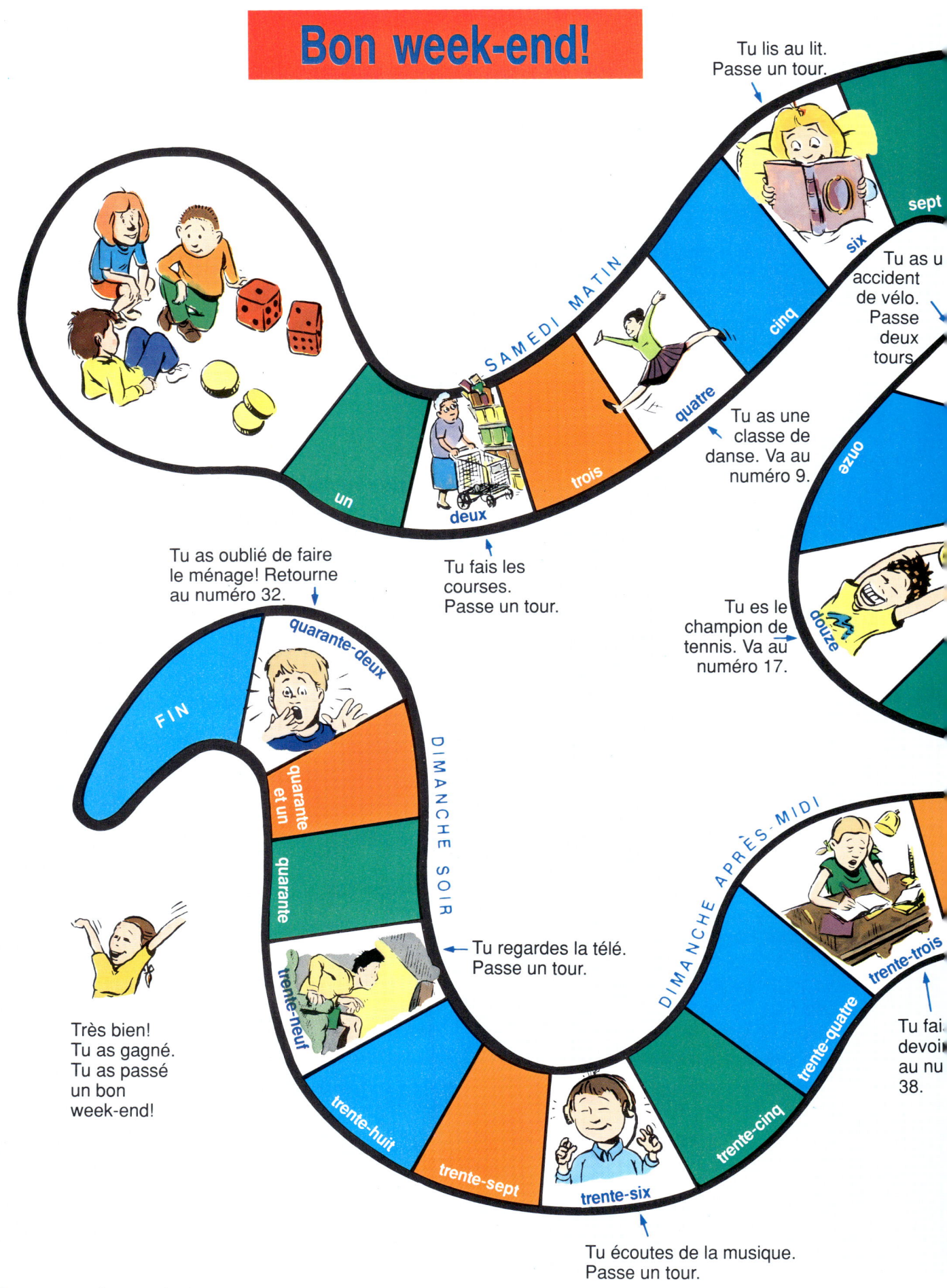

SAMEDI MATIN

- **un**
- **deux** — Tu fais les courses. Passe un tour.
- **trois**
- **quatre** — Tu as une classe de danse. Va au numéro 9.
- **cinq**
- **six** — Tu lis au lit. Passe un tour.
- **sept** — Tu as un accident de vélo. Passe deux tours.
- **onze**
- **douze** — Tu es le champion de tennis. Va au numéro 17.

DIMANCHE APRÈS-MIDI

- **trente-trois** — Tu fais tes devoirs. Va au numéro 38.
- **trente-quatre**
- **trente-cinq**
- **trente-six** — Tu écoutes de la musique. Passe un tour.
- **trente-sept**
- **trente-huit**

DIMANCHE SOIR

- **trente-neuf** — Tu regardes la télé. Passe un tour.
- **quarante**
- **quarante et un**
- **quarante-deux** — Tu as oublié de faire le ménage! Retourne au numéro 32.

FIN — Très bien! Tu as gagné. Tu as passé un bon week-end!

68 soixante-huit   Unité six

Joue le jeu du week-end! Prends un dé et des jetons et joue avec un, deux ou trois amis. Fais un six pour commencer.

ÉCOLE de DANSE

SAMEDI APRÈS-MIDI

SAMEDI SOIR

ROXY CINÉ

RETOUR AU FUTUR: Numéro 10

Tu vas au cinéma. Passe un tour.

dix-neuf
dix-huit
dix-sept
seize
quinze
quatorze

vingt
vingt et un
vingt-deux
vingt-trois
vingt-quatre
vingt-cinq
vingt-six
vingt-sept
vingt-huit
vingt-neuf
trente
trente et un

Les Misérables

DIMANCHE MATIN

STADE

Tu vas chez un ami jouer à des jeux vidéo. Tu arrives chez toi en retard. Retourne au numéro 7.

Tu fais la cuisine. Papa adore les éclairs au chocolat. Va au numéro 20.

Tu vas au théâtre. Va au numéro 21.

Tu fais la vaisselle. Maman est contente. Tu as un tour supplémentaire.

Tu écoutes la radio. Passe un tour.

Défense de plonger.

Tu joues au football. Tu as oublié ton maillot. Retourne au numéro 23.

Tu vas nager à la piscine. Va au numéro 31.

Unité six

soixante-neuf 69

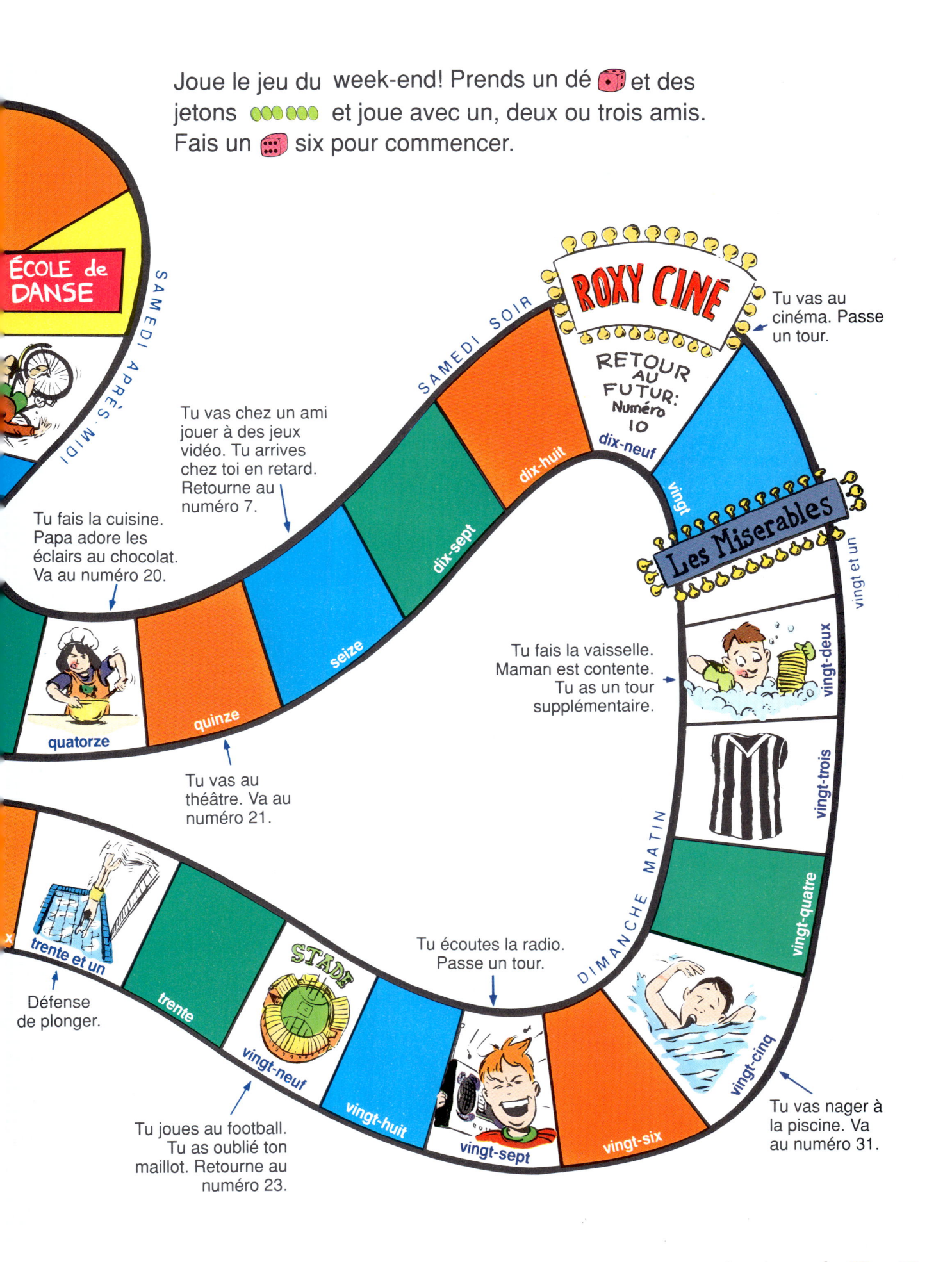

Vocabulaire

À LA MAISON

où est-ce que tu habites?	where do you live?
j'habite rue Pasteur	I live in Pasteur Street
chez moi, toi, Gilles	at my, your, Gilles' place
la chaîne stéréo	stereo system
la télévision	television
le chat	cat
le chien	dog
le poisson	fish
les courses	shopping
les devoirs	homework
les jeux vidéo	video games
le ménage	housework

C'EST BIEN LE MOT

comme	like
énorme	enormous
le joueur	player
magnifique	magnificent
le maillot	football shirt
la maison	house
le menteur	liar
le monde	world
passer	to call by
pendant	during
la personne	person
peut-être	maybe, perhaps
puis	then
la répétition	rehearsal
seulement	only
sur	on
la vie	life
vraiment	really

EXPRESSIONS UTILES

bien sûr	of course!
d'accord	OK, all right
dis donc	hey listen, tell me
en vacances	on holiday
on y va?	let's go?
pas grand-chose	not much
quelle barbe!	what a drag!
tout seul	all alone

QU'EST-CE QUE TU VAS FAIRE?

aider	to help
aller	to go
chanter	to sing
écouter	to listen (to)
jouer	to play
manger	to eat
nager	to swim
plonger	to dive
regarder	to look (at)
rester	to stay

LES SPORTS

le babyfoot	table football
la danse	dancing
le football	football
le tennis	tennis

EN VILLE

le cinéma	cinema
la piscine	swimming pool
la salle de jeux	games arcade
le terrain de tennis	tennis court
le théâtre	theatre

LE WEEK-END

vendredi soir	Friday evening
samedi matin	Saturday morning
dimanche après-midi	Sunday afternoon
demain, c'est lundi	tomorrow is Monday

Quel progrès!

Félicitations! Now you can do all these things in French!

- say what you like doing
- say what you're going to do
- ask what someone's going to do
- say what someone's going to do
- ask where people live
- say where you live
- say where other people live
- talk about what you have at home
- invite people to your place

Regardez maintenant: les fiches I1, I2 et I3

UNITÉ SEPT
Allons à Paris

Dimanche matin, chez Paul. Paul est très content parce qu'aujourd'hui la famille Richard va à Paris.

1. Et maintenant je vais parler avec le nouveau champion de planche à roulettes, Paul Richard. Bonjour, Paul. Tu es vraiment en forme aujourd'hui.

   Qu'est-ce que tu fais, Paul? Pourquoi est-ce que tu parles tout seul?

   Ah oui, ça, c'est normal.

2. Odette, ma petite sœur, ton frère est un champion. Regarde mon bras! Je suis bien musclé!

   Mais tu n'as pas grand-chose dans la tête.

3. Qu'est-ce qu'un champion prend le matin? Il prend du Chocolait.

4. Oui, je travaille beaucoup, et je joue beaucoup, mais avec le Chocolait, je suis toujours en forme.

5. Mon frère est fou, il est vraiment fou!

   Vite, Paul. Ton père est dans la voiture.

Unité sept — soixante-douze — 71

6. La famille Richard arrive au Palais de Chaillot. Monsieur Richard porte le parasol et le bébé. Madame Richard porte le pique-nique et Paul porte sa planche à roulettes.

7.
— Odette, qu'est-ce que tu fais?
— Je cherche la crème solaire, maman.
— Ah, voilà la crème. Mais où est Paul? Il oublie toujours la crème solaire!

8.
— Paul, viens ici! Un peu sur le visage...le nez... ferme les yeux, Paul.
— Et les oreilles, maman. Tu oublies toujours les oreilles.

9.
— Et toi, tu parles trop!
— Voilà, c'est tout! Vas-y.
— Ah non! Pas sur la bouche!

10.
— Bonjour! Je suis ici pour le concours.
— Très bien. Comment t'appelles-tu?
— Je m'appelle Paul Richard.

72 soixante-douze   Unité sept

11. — Quel âge as-tu? — J'ai douze ans.

12. — Où habites-tu? — J'habite à Beaumont, au numéro vingt-huit, avenue de l'École. — Et tu fais bien de la planche à roulettes, n'est-ce pas?

13. — Oui, bien sûr, je fais très bien... — D'accord. Voilà, pour toi, c'est le numéro soixante-dix-sept.

14. — Sandrine!?! Qu'est-ce que tu fais ici? — Pas grand-chose. Et toi?

15. — Je suis ici pour le concours de planche à roulettes. Tu parles avec le nouveau champion.

16. — Ah bon? Bonne chance, alors.

Regardez maintenant: les fiches A1 et A2.

Unité sept soixante-treize 73

Parlons

Série Un

1. Qu'est-ce que tu fais?
2. Je fais mes devoirs.
3. Pourquoi est-ce que tu écoutes de la musique?
4. Parce que j'aime faire mes devoirs et écouter de la musique.

Pour utiliser chaque expression avec chaque dessin, changez les mots en italique.

1.

2. J'adore *l'école.*

3.

A Et *Sandrine*, qu'est-ce qu'*elle* fait?

Elle parle avec Paul, et *elle porte sa planche à roulettes.*

4.

B Qu'est-ce que tu fais, *Gilles*?

Je mange et *j'écoute de la musique.*

C *Roger*, pourquoi est-ce que tu *travailles*?

Je travaille parce que j'aime *travailler.*

5.

Regardez maintenant: les fiches B1, B2 et B3

74 soixante-quatorze   Unité sept

Parlons

Série Deux

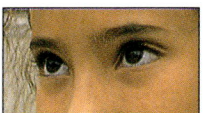

1 les yeux
2 la tête 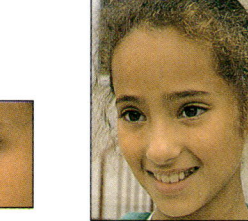
3 le corps 
4 la jambe 
5 les cheveux 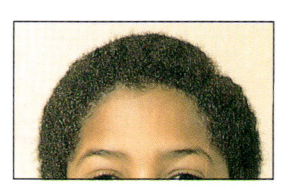
6 le visage 
7 l'oreille 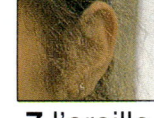
8 le pied 
9 la bouche 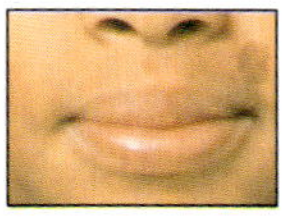
10 le ventre 
11 le bras 
12 la main 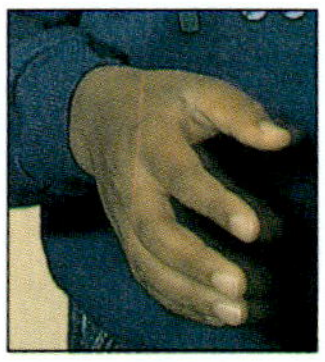
13 le nez 

Pour utiliser chaque expression avec chaque partie du dessin, changez les mots en italique.

A Où *sont les yeux*?
   Voilà *les yeux*!

B Où *est la tête*?
   La tête est ici.

Regardez maintenant: les fiches C1 et C2

Unité sept   soixante-quinze 75

Parlons

Série Trois

1. Qui est-ce, Isabelle?
2. C'est mon père, mon frère, ma mère, ma soeur... et mon chien.
3. Comment s'appelle ton frère?
4. Il s'appelle Fabien.

Pour utiliser chaque expression avec les differentes personnes dans le dessin, changez les mots en italique.

A	Qui est-ce, *Paul*?
	C'est *mon père*.

B	Comment s'appelle *ta femme, Bertrand*?
	Elle s'appelle *Marie-Louise*.

C	*Odette* a combien de *frères*?
	Elle a *deux frères*.

Odette Paul Bertrand François Marie-Louise

Regardez maintenant: les fiches D1, D2 et D3

76 soixante-seize

Unité sept

Parlons... avec un(e) partenaire

*Moi, je suis **A**. Toi, tu es **B**.*

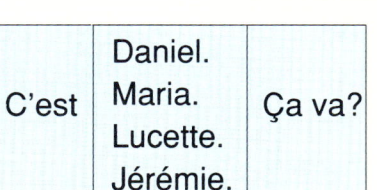

D'accord.

A | Allô.

B | Allô. Bonjour. Bonsoir. | Qui est-ce?

A | C'est | Daniel. Maria. Lucette. Jérémie. | Ça va?

B | Ah oui, ça va. Ça va bien, merci. | Qu'est-ce que tu fais maintenant?

A | Moi, | je / j' | joue au Monopoly / regarde la télé / fais la vaisselle / écoute de la musique | avec | ma mère. / mon père.

B | Pourquoi est-ce que tu | regardes la télé? / joues au Monopoly? / fais la vaisselle? / écoutes de la musique?

A | Parce que j'aime | regarder la télé. / jouer au Monopoly. / faire la vaisselle. / écouter de la musique.

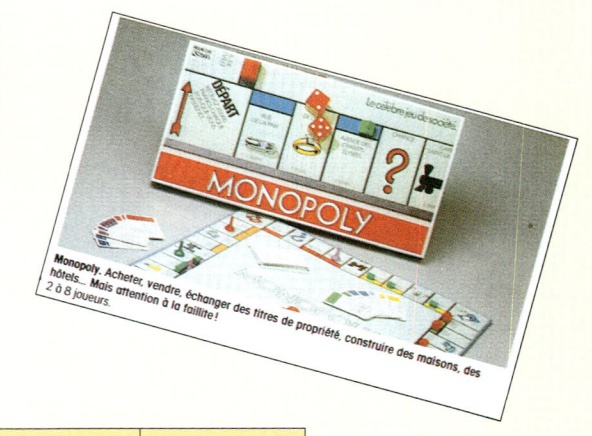

B | Moi, / Moi aussi, | je déteste / j'adore | ça.

Ton frère, / Ta soeur, | qu'est-ce qu' | il / elle | fait?

A | Il / Elle | est à | Paris / la piscine | pour | le concours de planche à roulettes. / un concours de natation.

B | Ah bon! | Il / Elle | a | les bras / le corps / les jambes | d' | un champion. / une championne.

Unité sept   soixante-dix-sept 77

| A | Tu crois? Dis donc! Est-ce que tu vas à | l'école / la piscine | demain? | | B | Oui, bien sûr. |

| A | N'oublie pas | ta crème solaire, mon jeu vidéo, le test, tes devoirs, | alors. | | B | D'accord! À demain! À bientôt! | | A | Au revoir. |

Parlons... en situation

1 L'ALBUM DE FAMILLE

It's time to look at some more photos. Some of you might like to bring in some snaps of your family or friends. When you talk about them, you should be able to:

- say where you live
- give some information about your house
- point out family members, including pets, and say what relation they are to you (brother, mother etc.)
- give their names and ages
- say what they usually do (e.g. sport, hobbies)

If you're doing really well, you might like to give some extra information about the people in the photos.

e.g.

Mon père	**travaille**	dans un bureau (an office). dans une usine (a factory). dans une école. à la maison.
Ma soeur		

When someone else is showing their photos, you should be able to ask the right questions to find out the above information.

2 TU CONNAIS TON AMI(E)?

Make up ten questions for a friend of yours, making use of the verbs we have been practising in this unit, and try to predict whether your friend will answer **oui** or **non** to each of them. Write the questions down with your prediction next to each one. Now ask your friend each question.
At the end you'll see just how well you know each other.
Here are some examples of questions you could ask.

Tu habites à Moss Side?
Tu aides ta mère?
Tu nages bien?
Tu aimes le chocolat?

Regardez maintenant: les fiches E1 et E2

soixante-dix-huit   Unité sept

Ça c'est le français

FRENCH VERBS - THE PRESENT TENSE

The *present tense* of a verb tells what is happening at the present time.

e.g. **Je cherche la crème solaire.**
I'm looking for the suntan cream.

Don't confuse expressions such as I am looking (**Je cherche**) with those such as I am intelligent (**Je suis intelligent(e)**).

The present tense is also used to express what usually or always happens.

e.g. **Tu oublies toujours la crème solaire.**
You always forget the suntan cream.

The present tense is also used to express commands or requests.

e.g. **Gilles, ouvre le livre!**
Gilles, open the book!
Désirée, ferme la porte!
Désirée, close the door.

What do you notice about the sound of the **je**, **tu**, **il** and **elle** forms of the verbs in the box below? What spelling change do you have to be careful of?

So as not to complicate things too much we have been concentrating on the largest group of French verbs, those that have the *infinitive* (the part that means to...) ending in **-er**.

All **-er** verbs (except one!) follow the pattern we have seen in this chapter. Here are the ones we have used so far.

aider	to help	**manger**	to eat
aimer	to like, love	**nager**	to swim
arriver	to arrive	**oublier**	to forget
chanter	to sing	**parler**	to speak, talk
chercher	to look for		
danser	to dance	**porter**	to carry
détester	to hate	**regarder**	to look (at), watch
écouter	to listen (to)		
habiter	to live	**travailler**	to work
jouer	to play		

Regardez maintenant: la fiche F1

PARLER
Maintenant je parle avec Paul Richard.
Pourquoi est-ce que tu parles tout seul?
Il est fou; il parle tout seul.
Elle est folle; elle parle toute seule.

TO SPEAK
Now I'm speaking to Paul Richard.
Why are you talking to yourself.
He's crazy. He's talking to himself.
She's crazy. She's talking to herself.

TRAVAILLER
C'est vrai, je travaille beaucoup.
Est-ce que tu travailles tous les week-ends?
Bien sûr, il travaille toujours.
Bien sûr, elle travaille toujours.

TO WORK
It's true, I work hard.
Do you work every weekend?
Of course, he always works.
Of course, she always works.

Unité sept

Rendez-vous par ordinateur

Roger has programmed Robobot so that he can match you with the perfect friend. All you have to do is to fill in the form on Repromaster G1, and the information can then be fed into the computer.
Paul has already filled in the one below to give you the idea.

♥ Comment t'appelles-tu? Paul Richard

♥ Quel âge as-tu? J'ai douze ans.

♥ Matière préférée le français.
Chanson préférée "J'adore l'école".
Équipe préférée Beaumont
Groupe préféré Les Chiens Moches.
Émission de télé préférée "Les Voisins".
Sport préféré le tennis.

♥ Qu'est-ce que tu as chez toi? (cochez)

un chat ☐
un chien ☐
un poisson rouge ☑
un ordinateur ☐
une piscine ☐
un terrain de tennis ☐

♥ Est-ce que tu es...
belle/beau? Oui, je suis beau.
moche? Non, je ne suis pas moche.
sympa? Oui, je suis sympa.
fort(e)? Oui, je suis fort.
intelligent(e)? Je ne suis pas très intelligent.
menteuse/menteur? Je suis un grand menteur.
riche? Oui, je suis riche.
sportive/sportif? Bien sûr!

♥ Description de ton/ta partenaire idéal(e).

Ma partenaire idéale est très sympa. Elle a les cheveux blonds et les yeux bleus. Elle n'est pas bête, elle est très intelligente. Elle joue au football et elle adore aller au cinéma.

Regardez maintenant: la fiche G1

quatre-vingts

Unité sept

La Belle France

LES FRONTIÈRES DE LA FRANCE

Study the map and you'll see that most of France's borders with other countries are well defined by natural geographical features. What separates France from England? How is France divided from Spain? What is the natural barrier between France and its neighbouring countries, Italy and Switzerland? How would you know you have crossed from France into Germany?

France is in a very central position in Western Europe, isn't it? No wonder it has played a major role in the most important events in European history.

Notice that the map of France includes the island of **Corse** (Corsica), which lies about 160 kilometres off the mainland. Which famous Frenchman grew up on this island?

Unité sept quatre-vingt-un 81

LES MONTAGNES ET LES RIVIÈRES

Look at the map again and pay particular attention to the mountainous areas that are marked on it. Now imagine that you have a bird's eye view of the whole of France and you'll see that the country is shaped like an open-air stadium. Centre stage, on the flat, is the city of Paris with the tiers of 'seats' rising away to the south and west.

As you head away from the northern plains around the capital you come to the first raised areas, **les Vosges** and **le Jura** mountains in the east and the central highland area known as **le Massif Central.**

The further you get from the 'stage' the higher you go: **les Pyrénées** to the south-west and **les Alpes** to the south-east. **Le Mont Blanc** is in the Alps. At 4,807 metres it is the highest mountain in Europe. How does this compare with the highest mountains in Scotland and Wales?

The great rivers of France rise in these mountainous areas and flow away towards the sea. By studying the map you should be able to work out which river starts where.

The longest river is **la Loire**, which flows for 1,000 kilometres. How does this compare with Britain's longest rivers?

In the 1500s the valley of the Loire River became the fashionable place for members of the French royal and noble families to build their **châteaux**. This one is called **Chenonceaux**.

This **deux chevaux** car really looks at home in this old part of Strasbourg, doesn't it? Do you know what special importance this city has for the European Community? Strasbourg is not a very French-sounding name, is it?

In the 1200s some very daring monks chose this rocky outcrop off the Atlantic coast to build their monastery. It's called **Mont St Michel**. Those sheep had better not get much closer or they'll get stuck in the quicksand that surrounds it.

As well as its great rivers, France has a network of canals plied by **les péniches** - barges like this one. Some French people make canal transport a way of life and actually live on barges. And you can have a great holiday if you hire one. When you need some exercise you can ride a bike along the towpath.

Regardez maintenant: la fiche H1

quatre-vingt-deux

Unité sept

Learning about language

FRENCH AND ENGLISH ARE RELATED

We have already noticed that there are lots of similarities between French and English.

To understand why, we need to go back just over two thousand years to the Roman invasion of Gaul, as France was known in those days. Despite the brave exploits of Asterix and Obélix, Julius Caesar conquered the Gauls in 51 B.C.

As the Romans spread their Empire across Gaul into Spain and Britain, they took their language with them. The language of these ancient Romans is called Latin. No one has Latin as their main language any more, but in those days the people conquered by the Romans were proud to become Roman citizens and to learn Latin. Modern French, Spanish and Italian are descended from this ancient language of the Romans, and English was heavily influenced by it.

Latin is now regarded as a dead language, but in a certain sense it is very much alive. For example, the Latin word for foot was **pede**, the French word is **pied**, the Italian is **piede** and the Spanish **pie**. English has words such as pedal and pedestrian which are derived from the Latin. (On Repromaster I1 you will find a table to fill in with similar examples.)

Regardez maintenant: la fiche I1

Unité sept

quatre-vingt-trois 83

Leçon • Les sons • Leçon • Les sons • Leçon

As well as getting individual vowel and consonant sounds right, if you really want to sound French you have to get the rhythm of the language, you have to get the beat.

You may not have noticed before, but when you are speaking English you give words, phrases and sentences a certain rhythm by putting stress or emphasis on certain syllables. Try it out by saying these lines:

Hooray, hooray!! Let's get away, and explore the land across the bay.

You should find that you are stressing the final syllable in each word or in each group of words.

English doesn't always have this sort of beat, but this is the rhythm of French. In French, make sure you put the beat on the final syllable. Practise by saying these words.

Paris, français, maman, ménage, devoirs, formidable, fantastique, babyfoot, ordinateur, professeur

Now practise these:

**Bonjour, monsieur.
Merci beaucoup.
Je parle anglais.
Je vais nager.
Le nouveau champion.
Bonne chance, alors!
Tu oublies toujours les oreilles.**

Concentrate on getting the right beat whenever you are speaking French.

LES SPORTS D'HIVER A... GÉRARDMER
FRANCE VOSGES

L'APRES-SKI

Casino : tous les jours en soirée, aux week-ends et fêtes.
Maison de la Culture : nombreuses activités et spectacles, expositions.
Cinéma : Salle du Casino, Salle de la M.C.L. classée "Art et Essai".
Discothèques :
* "La Chaumière", La Basse-des-Rupts,
* "New-York City", 8, place Albert Ferry
* "Le Pacific", place Albert Ferry
* "Le Jackpot", quai du Lac,
* "Le News", 13, rue de la Gare
* "La Soyotte", Les Pergis, à Xonrupt,
* "L'Excuse", 6, rue de la Gare Tél. 29 63 43 34
* "La Chaumière", La Basse-des-Rupts Tél. 29 63 05 69

**Bar d'ambiance
Restaurant de nuit

Salle de Squash** rue Carnot Prolongée. Tous les jours de 10 à 22 heures. Deux pistes. Tél. 29 63 44 76
Expositions artistiques et d'artisanat : Salle de la Maison de l'Artisanat, Place du Vieux Gérardmer, et Maison de la Culture et des Loisirs.
Jeux : Jeux électriques, rue de la Gare. Bowling, complexe piscine-patinoire, quai du Locle, tél. 29 63 18 31.
Billard : Etage de l'Hôtel du Tilleul - rue des Vosges. Le Neptune - Av. de Vichy.
Bibliothèque Municipale : Rue de la Promenade (fermée le vendredi).
Service de Baby-sitting : informations auprès de la M.C.L., tél. 29 63 11 96.
Loto : enregistrement à : "La Civette", rue de la Gare - "Au Cadran", place du Tilleul - "Le Rénitas", 35, boulevard Kelsch.
P.M.U. : jours de tiercé de 9 h à 11 h 45, au Palais de la Bière, rue de la Gare.
Radio locale : 99,1 Mhz, FM2.

Vocabulaire

C'EST BIEN LE MOT!

allô	hello? (when answering the phone)
le bureau	office
le champion	champion
la championne	champion
le concours	competition
la crème solaire	suntan cream
ma, mon	my
la planche à roulettes	skateboard
prendre	to have, take
le rendez-vous	meeting, date
ta, ton	your
la voiture	car

LA FAMILLE

le bébé	baby
la famille	family
la femme	woman, wife
la fille	girl, daughter
le fils	son
le frère	brother
la mère	mother
le mari	husband
le père	father
la sœur	sister

Simon dit, "Touchez le nez!"

EXPRESSIONS UTILES

bonne chance!	good luck!
c'est tout!	that's all
être en forme	to be in form
où sont?	where are?
tu crois?	do you think so?
un peu	a little
vas-y!	go ahead!

LE CORPS

la bouche	mouth
le bras	arm
les cheveux (m)	hair
le corps	body
la jambe	leg
la main	hand
le nez	nose
l'oeil (m)	eye
l'oreille (f)	ear
le pied	foot
la tête	head
le ventre	stomach
le visage	face
les yeux (m)	eyes

Quel progrès!

Félicitations! Now you can do all these things in French!

- ask what someone is doing
- say what you're doing
- say what someone else is doing
- identify parts of the body
- identify family members

Regardez maintenant: les fiches J1, J2 et J3

Unité sept   quatre-vingt-cinq   85

UNITÉ HUIT
Le concours

1. C'est le 22 juin. Au Palais de Chaillot, à Paris, il y a un grand concours de planche à roulettes.

Mesdames, Messieurs, bienvenue au Palais de Chaillot. Quel spectacle, Christine!

Oui, Pascal. Les concurrents, les spectateurs, la Tour Eiffel ...quelle atmosphère!

Oui, ça bouge! Et il fait beau aujourd'hui.

Oui. Il y a du soleil, mais il fait un peu froid.

2. C'est vrai, Christine. Le vent est un peu froid mais on est seulement en juin. C'est l'été, mais c'est seulement la première semaine.

Moi, j'adore l'été. Je déteste l'hiver.

3. Oui, Christine, on aime tous l'été, le soleil, la planche à roulettes...les mouches.

Et voilà le prochain concurrent, numéro soixante-dix-sept. Qui est-ce, Pascal?

4. Il s'appelle Paul Richard. Il a douze ans. Il est né à Etretat, mais maintenant il habite Beaumont.

5. Regarde, Pascal. Paul fait un tour très difficile sur sa planche à roulettes. Quel casse-cou!

86 quatre-vingt-six · Unité huit

6.

7.
- Mon Dieu!
- Je suis désolé.
- Qu'est-ce que tu fais? Tu es fou!

8.
- Et maintenant une concurrente, numéro quatre-vingt-onze. C'est la dernière concurrente. Comment s'appelle-t-elle, Christine?
- Elle s'appelle Sandrine Lagarde. On a quatre concurrentes au Palais de Chaillot aujourd'hui, Pascal.
- C'est intéressant, Christine. Alors on va peut-être avoir une championne, cet été. Sandrine est très forte et elle est très élégante.

9.
- C'est vrai, Pascal. Elle est née à la Martinique et maintenant elle habite Beaumont. Elle fait très bien de la planche à roulettes.

10.
- Elle a du style. Et maintenant c'est la fin, je crois. On attend les résultats...

11.
- Mesdames, Messieurs, votre attention, s'il vous plaît. Le nouveau champion... euh...c'est-à-dire, la nouvelle championne est...Sandrine Lagarde.
- Voilà la coupe, Sandrine. Et voici le prix: un voyage pour deux à la Guadeloupe.

Unité huit — quatre-vingt-sept — 87

12.
— Mince! Il pleut! Où est le parapluie, Pascal. Tu oublies toujours le parapluie.
— Tais-toi, Christine! J'interviewe Sandrine. Quand est-ce que tu vas à la Guadeloupe, Sandrine?

13.
— Je ne sais pas. En août, peut-être. Il fait chaud pendant toute l'année en Guadeloupe, n'est-ce pas?

14.
— Mademoiselle Sandrine, un grand sourire pour la presse.
— Dis donc, Sandrine, tu ne fais pas grand-chose aujourd'hui, hein?

15.
— Je suis désolée, Paul.

16.
— Désolée? Pourquoi? Je n'ai pas envie d'être une vedette, moi.

17. Le lendemain matin.
— Ohé les gars! Ma photo est dans le journal.

Regardez maintenant: les fiches A1 et A2.

88 quatre-vingt-huit — Unité huit

Parlons

Série Un

1. Est-ce que tu vas aller au cinéma avec moi?
2. Oui, d'accord. Quel jour?
3. Mardi premier... ou mercredi ou jeudi.
4. Euh...mardi, je crois.

Pour utiliser chaque expression avec le calendrier, changez les mots en italique.

A Aujourd'hui c'est le 17.

   Alors, c'est *jeudi*.

B Quand est-ce que tu vas *jouer au tennis*?

   Euh...*lundi sept*, je crois.

Les jours de la semaine
lundi
mardi
mercredi
jeudi
vendredi
samedi
dimanche

Regardez maintenant: les fiches B1, B2 et B3

Unité huit — quatre-vingt-neuf 89

Parlons

Série Deux

1. Mmm...Biarritz... on est en quelle saison, au printemps?
2. Mais non! On est en été.
3. Est-ce qu'il fait beau en été?
4. Ah, oui. Il fait beau. Et il ne pleut pas! À Biarritz, il pleut en automne et en hiver.

Pour utiliser chaque expression avec chaque dessin, changez les mots en italique.

1 Il fait du vent.
2 Il fait beau. 
3 Il pleut. 
4 Il fait chaud. 
5 Il fait mauvais. Il gèle. 
6 Il fait froid. Il neige. 

A Est-ce qu'il *fait beau*?
   ou
   Est-ce qu'il *pleut*?

   Oui, il *fait beau*.
   ou
   Non, il ne *pleut* pas.

B On est en quelle saison?

   On est *en été*, je crois.

C Est-ce que tu aimes *l'hiver*?

   Moi, j'adore *l'hiver*.
   ou
   Moi, je déteste *l'hiver*.

Regardez maintenant: les fiches C1, C2 et C3

quatre-vingt-dix   Unité huit

Parlons

Série Trois

1. Quand est-ce que tu vas aller en Australie? 
2. En décembre, je crois.
3. Et quand est-ce que tu rentres au Canada?
4. Je vais rentrer au Canada en février.

Pour utiliser chaque expression avec chaque brochure, changez les mots en italique.

Les mois de l'année
janvier
février
mars
avril
mai
juin
juillet
août
septembre
octobre
novembre
décembre

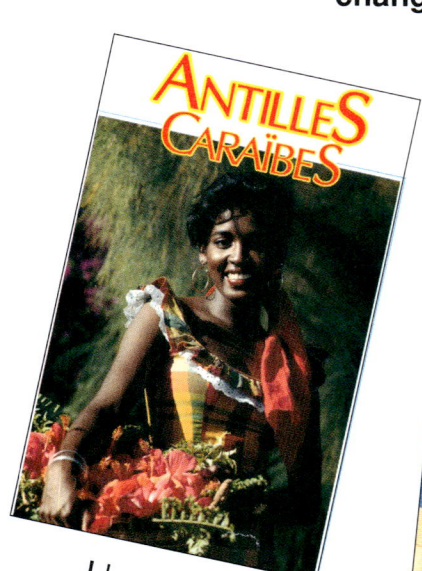

ANTILLES CARAÏBES
Un voyage aux Antilles

Allez en Thaïlande

Croisière en Egypte

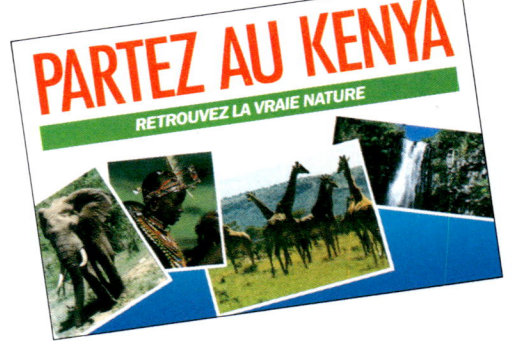

PARTEZ AU KENYA
RETROUVEZ LA VRAIE NATURE

Des vacances en GRANDE BRETAGNE

A Où est-ce que tu vas aller?
Je vais aller *au Kenya*.

B Quand est-ce que tu vas rentrer *en Grande-Bretagne*?
Je vais rentrer en *août*.

Regardez maintenant: les fiches D1, D2, D3 et D4

Unité huit — quatre-vingt-onze — 91

Parlons... avec un(e) partenaire

Moi, je suis **A**. Toi, tu es **B**.

D'accord.

| A | Allô. |

| B | Allô. Ah, | Ali, Annie, Géraldine, Nicolas, | c'est toi. | Tu es où Où es-tu | cette semaine? aujourd'hui? maintenant? |

| A | Oui, c'est moi. | Aujourd'hui, Maintenant, Cette semaine, | je suis on est | en | Italie. Espagne. Turquie. France. |

| B | Ah bon! Ça alors! | Quel temps fait-il en | Italie Espagne Turquie France | aujourd'hui? |

| A | Il fait | beau. du vent. mauvais. du soleil. | Il fait | un peu chaud. très chaud. vraiment froid. |

| B | C'est quelle saison en Europe? Ici en Nouvelle-Calédonie, il fait toujours chaud! |

| A | On est | en hiver. en automne. en été. au printemps. | C'est le | premier vingt-cinq treize trente | janvier, juillet, octobre, avril, | n'est-ce pas? |

| B | Moi, j'aime | l'été. l'hiver. le printemps. l'automne. | J'aime J'adore Je déteste | le soleil. la plage. les mouches. le vent froid. la pluie. | Et comment va | ta la | famille? |

92 quatre-vingt-douze   Unité huit

| A | Pas mal.
Très bien, merci.
Ça bouge. | Demain on va | au
en | Portugal.
Suisse.
Belgique.
Grèce. |

| B | Quand est-ce que tu | vas rentrer
rentres | en Nouvelle-Calédonie? |

| A | La semaine prochaine.
Le 12 août.
En juillet.
En hiver. |

| B | Bon voyage, alors! | | A | Merci. Au revoir. |

Parlons... en situation

L'ÉMISSION SPORTIVE

Team up with somebody to present a radio broadcast of your school sports for the millions of interested listeners in France. You'll think of lots of things to say, but be sure to include the following in your broadcast.
- Introduce yourselves to the listeners and welcome them to the sports **(le meeting d'athlétisme)**.
- Describe the scene and have an informative discussion about the weather.
- Introduce and describe some of the competitors.
- Announce the results and interview the winner.

QUEL TEMPS FAIT-IL?

Make up and act out a telephone conversation with someone living abroad. The main part of your conversation will be about the weather. Ask each other about local conditions and give detailed and informative answers.

Regardez maintenant: les fiches E1 et E2

Unité huit

Ça c'est le français

1 ON

The easiest French word for <u>we</u> is **on**. With **on** you use the same part of the different verbs as you do for **il** and **elle**.

e.g. **En Écosse, on aime beaucoup l'été.**
In Scotland, we really like summer.
On ne joue pas avec toi.
We're not playing with you.

Notice that **on** can mean <u>we</u> in the very broad general sense of <u>all of us in Scotland</u> (as in the first example), and in the more restricted sense of <u>my friend and I</u> (as in the second example).

2 FAIRE

a) The verb **faire** (<u>to do</u>, <u>to make</u>) is very important in French because it is used in so many different expressions. Notice that it does not follow exactly the same pattern as **-er** verbs such as **jouer** and **aimer**.

> **Je fais la vaisselle.**
> **Qu'est-ce que tu fais?**
> **Il fait un tour difficile.**
> **Elle fait un jeu vidéo.**
> **On fait un concours de planche à roulettes.**
>
> I'm washing up.
> What are you doing?
> He's doing a difficult trick.
> She's playing a video game.
> We're having a roller-skating competition.

b) **Il fait**, a part of the verb **faire**, is used in many weather expressions.

il fait beau	it's lovely weather
il fait mauvais	it's awful weather
il fait du vent	it's windy
il fait du soleil	it's sunny
il fait froid	it's cold
il fait chaud	it's hot

3 LES SAISONS

l'été	summer
l'hiver	winter
l'automne	autumn
le printemps	spring

To say <u>in</u> with the seasons, you say

> **en été**
> **en hiver**
> **en automne** but
> **au printemps**

4 NAMES OF COUNTRIES

In French, the names of most countries are *feminine*.

la Grèce	Greece
la Belgique	Belgium
l'Écosse (f)	Scotland

To say <u>in</u> or <u>to</u> these countries, you say:

> **Je suis née en Égypte.**
> I was born in Egypt.
> **Je vais en Chine.**
> I'm going to China.

But some countries have *masculine* names.

le Sénégal	Senegal
le Japon	Japan
le Portugal	Portugal

To say <u>in</u> or <u>to</u> these countries you say:

> **Au Pakistan, il fait chaud.**
> It's hot in Pakistan.
> **Tu rentres au Vietnam?**
> Are you going back to Vietnam?

Where a country is really a collection of islands or states, its name is often *plural*.

les Antilles	the West Indies
les Îles Anglo-Normandes	the Channel Islands

In this case, you say:

> **Un voyage aux Antilles**
> A trip to the West Indies
> **Je suis né aux États-Unis.**
> I was born in the United States.

> Regardez maintenant: la fiche F1

Unité huit

Learning about language

POSITIVE LISTENING!

Most of the advice given about developing your reading skills in French also applies to listening skills. Above all, focus on what you do understand and don't be put off by what you don't.

There are some people who have a problem with a word or two and give up in despair. (Not you, of course!) What they should be doing is using what they can grasp as clues to help fill in the gaps. Don't just go word by word, go with the flow. After all, this is what we all do when we are listening to English. We often miss words here and there, but that doesn't stop us getting the overall meaning of what is being said.

Asking people to repeat things is a normal part of everyday conversation.

Listen for the particular information that you need, and don't let yourself be distracted by all the other words being spoken around it. For example, if you're listening for numbers, concentrate all your attention on those; as far as you're concerned, the rest is just padding.

You have probably worked it out for yourself by now - intelligent guessing is one of the most important skills for a foreign language student to develop. And the other thing is to act confident, even when you don't feel it. This is exactly what the people who seem to understand everything are doing.

POSITIVE READING SKILLS II

The advice you have just been given probably reminds you of what was said on page 67. Why not reread that section now and then try putting theory into practice on this advertisement for an amusement park on the French Riviera. **Bonne lecture**!

OUVERT D'AVRIL A OCTOBRE

NICE ST ISIDORE ROUTE DE DIGNE

50 shows et animations, attractions géantes et attractions nautiques dont :

une piscine géante avec des vagues époustouflantes, 8 totoboggans aquatiques, des attractions géantes, 2 théâtres, des rivières à dévaler, un funiculaire!... et tout est compris dans le prix d'entrée.
11 restaurants (traditionnels, fast-foods et une cafétéria au bord du lac), 8 boutiques.

Tél. 93.18.36.36

90.3 FM / 95.4 FM RMC CÔTE D'AZUR
La radio du parc

ZYGOFOLIS
INTERNATIONAL CÔTE D'AZUR PARK

Unité huit   quatre-vingt-quinze   95

Ici on parle français:

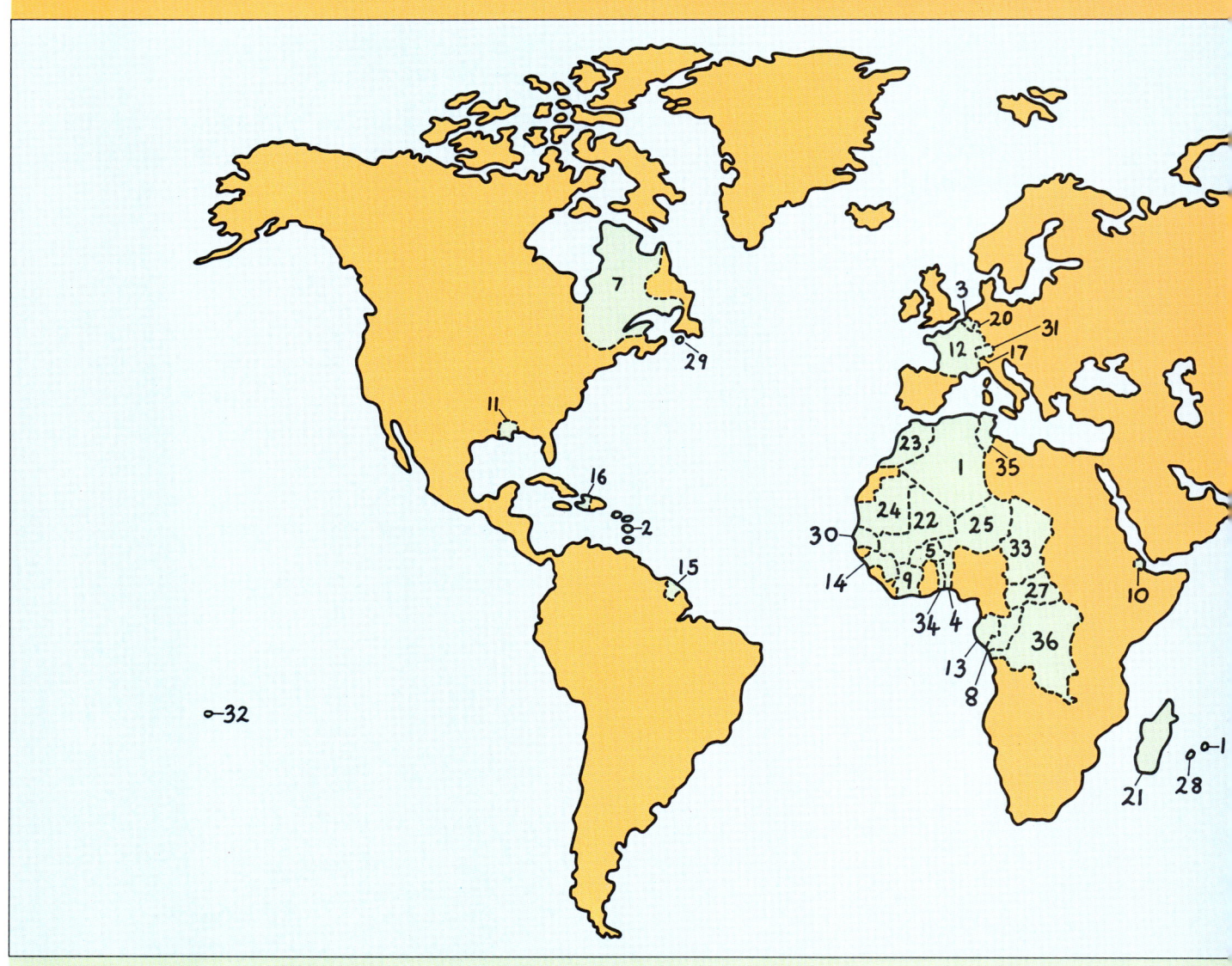

Ils parlent français et ...

Salut! Je suis Céline Je viens du Québec, au Canada. Je parle français et anglais.

Moi, je suis Mouda. J'habite au Cambodge. Je parle khmer et français.

Bonjour. Je m'appelle Abi. Je suis né en Côte d'Ivoire, en Afrique. Je parle malinke et français.

Bonjour. Je m'appelle Sita. Je suis née à l'Île Maurice, mais maintenant j'habite Belfast, en Irlande du Nord. Je parle hindi, français et anglais.

96 quatre-vingt-seize   Unité huit

Les pays francophones

Où est-ce qu'on parle français?
En France, bien sûr, mais dans beaucoup d'autres pays aussi.
Regardez la carte des pays francophones (les pays où on parle français).

On parle français dans trente-six pays et sur quatre continents: en Amérique, en Europe, en Afrique, et en Asie.

1. l'Algérie
2. les Antilles (la Guadeloupe, la Martinique, Saint-Martin)
3. la Belgique
4. le Bénin
5. le Burkina Faso
6. le Cambodge
7. le Canada (Québec)
8. le Congo
9. la Côte d'Ivoire
10. Djibouti
11. les États-Unis
12. la France
13. le Gabon
14. la Guinée
15. la Guyane
16. Haïti
17. l'Italie (Val d'Aoste)
18. l'Île Maurice
19. le Laos
20. le Luxembourg
21. la République Malgache
22. le Mali
23. le Maroc
24. la Mauritanie
25. le Niger
26. la Nouvelle-Calédonie
27. la République Centrafricaine
28. la Réunion
29. Saint-Pierre et Miquelon
30. le Sénégal
31. la Suisse
32. la Polynésie (Tahiti etc.)
33. le Tchad
34. le Togo
35. la Tunisie
36. le Zaïre

Leçon • Les sons • Leçon • Les sons • Leçon

You can really sound very French if you get the nasal sounds right. If you're having trouble with the sound in words such as **content** and **marrant** try saying <u>on</u> with your ordinary English accent, but don't let your tongue touch the roof of your mouth.

Here are some more sentences to practise with.

Et maintenant, un concurrent très élégant.
Quel temps! Quel vent!
Maman a trente ans.
Laurent Legrand est intelligent.

Make up some of your own to test a classmate!

Regardez maintenant: les fiches G1 et G2

Unité huit   quatre-vingt-dix-sept 97

Vocabulaire

LE TEMPS ET LES SAISONS

il fait beau	it's fine
il fait chaud	it's hot
il fait froid	it's cold
il fait mauvais	the weather's bad
il fait du soleil	it's sunny
il fait du vent	it's windy
il gèle	it's freezing
il neige	it's snowing
il pleut	it's raining
le printemps	spring
l'été(m)	summer
l'automne(m)	autumn
l'hiver(m)	winter

C'EST BIEN LE MOT

l'année(f)	year
attendre	to wait
difficile	difficult
le gars	guy
le journal	newspaper
le lendemain	the next day
libre	free
la mouche	fly
le parapluie	umbrella
la presse	press
prochain(e)	next
quand	when
quelqu'un	someone
rentrer	to go/come home
la semaine	week
le sourire	smile

LE CONCOURS

le casse-cou	daredevil
le, la concurrent(e)	competitor
la coupe	cup, trophy
dernière, dernier	last
première, premier	first
le prix	prize
le résultat	result
le spectateur	spectator
le tour	trick, stunt
la vedette	star

EXPRESSIONS UTILES

avoir du style	to be stylish
avoir envie de	to want
bon voyage!	have a good journey!
c'est vrai	that's right
elle est née	she was born
il est né	he was born
faire un tour difficile	to perform a difficult stunt
hein?	eh?
Mesdames, Messieurs	ladies and gentlemen
mince!	bother!

Quel progrès!

Félicitations! You are now able to use your French to do the following things.

- talk about the weather
- discuss the seasons
- say the day and the date
- say where you were born
- say what people like doing or are doing

Regardez maintenant: les fiches H1 et H2.

UNITÉ NEUF
On va au cinéma?

1．
- Mademoiselle Colbert, c'est presque la fin de l'année scolaire. On va faire quelque chose de spécial?
- Quelque chose de spécial?
- Oui, mademoiselle. La classe de Monsieur Ravel va voir les Chiens Moches à Paris.

2．
- Oui, et la classe d'anglais de Monsieur Baron va préparer un petit déjeuner à l'anglaise, avec des œufs au jambon et du thé.
- Beurk.

3．
- Et nous, qu'est-ce qu'on va faire?
- Oui, mademoiselle, qu'est-ce que nous allons faire?

4．
- Vous aimez aller au cinéma? Il y a un très bon film cette semaine. *Cendrillon*.
- Beurk. Quelle barbe! C'est pour les enfants, ça.

5．
- Mais il y a aussi *Dracula visite Frankenstein*. Ça, c'est chouette.

6．
- Alors, vous aimez les films d'horreur?
- Mais oui, bien sûr.

7．
- Mais vous n'avez pas peur?

Unité neuf — quatre-vingt-dix-neuf 99

8. Non, nous n'avons pas peur. On adore les films d'horreur.

9. D'accord, allons voir *Dracula visite*...etc.
Mademoiselle, fermez les yeux pendant le film si vous avez peur.

10. J'ai faim, moi. Qu'est-ce qu'on va manger? On va prendre un hamburger?
Oui, chouette! Extra! Formidable!

11. Non, merci, pas de fast food. Je déteste les hamburgers. Voyons...il y a un café par ici? Ah oui, voilà!
D'accord!!

12. On va manger ici en plein air? Ce n'est pas mal.
Oui. Il fait chaud aujourd'hui.

13. D'accord. Monsieur... s'il vous plaît.

14. Vous désirez?
Je voudrais un croissant au jambon.
Nous n'avons pas de croissants, aujourd'hui.

15. Alors, un sandwich au fromage sans beurre.
Pas de sandwichs!

16. Alors, je prends une crêpe à la confiture de fraise.
Pas de crêpes!

100 cent

Unité neuf

17.
— Pardon, monsieur. Qu'est-ce qu'il y a à manger, alors?
— Nous avons des hamburgers.

18.
— Chouette! Je prends un cheeseburger.
— Moi aussi.
— Moi aussi. Miam! Miam!

19.
— Et vous, mademoiselle?
— Alors, un cheeseburger, mais pas de fromage!

20.
— Un cheeseburger sans fromage!?! D'accord.
— Et pas de viande! Je n'aime pas ça. Et sans sauce. Je déteste la sauce.

21.
— C'est tout, mademoiselle?
— Oui...euh, et pas de pain. Je suis au régime. Mais je prends tout le reste.

22.
— Moi, j'ai soif. Qu'est-ce que vous avez comme boisson, monsieur?
— Comme boisson nous avons thé, café, chocolat chaud et jus d'orange.

23.
— Je prends un chocolat chaud.
— Moi aussi.

24.
— Et vous, mademoiselle? Un chocolat chaud sans chocolat?
— Mmm, non, merci. Je prends un jus d'orange.

25.
— Bon appétit!
— Euh...merci.

Unité neuf

cent un 101

26.
— Ça fait combien?
— Trente-deux francs quatre-vingts, s'il vous plaît, mademoiselle.
— Voilà, monsieur. Merci.
— Vite, mademoiselle. Le film commence tout de suite.

27.
— Pauvre Mademoiselle Colbert! Elle a peur.

28.
— O-o-o-oh! J'ai peur.
— Mia-ouou!
— Miam-miam!

29.
— Qu'est-ce que vous avez comme boisson?

30.
— Fantastique! Allons manger quelque chose. Un pain au chocolat, un sandwich, une crêpe...?

31.
— Non, merci. Nous n'avons pas faim, maintenant.

32.
— Je ne comprends pas. Les jeunes d'aujourd'hui n'ont pas d'appétit.

Regardez maintenant: les fiches A1 et A2.

cent deux

Unité neuf

Parlons

Série Un

1. Monsieur, s'il vous plaît!
2. Oui, Messieurs, Mesdames, vous désirez?
3. Deux cafés, deux chocolats chauds, et des croissants, s'il vous plaît.
4. Et vous, monsieur, qu'est-ce que vous prenez?
5. Mmm... j'ai soif, moi. Je prends du thé.
6. J'ai faim. Je voudrais du pain et de la confiture.

Pour utiliser chaque expression avec chaque photo, changez les mots en italique.

A Qu'est-ce qu'il y a pour le petit déjeuner?

Aujourd'hui il y a *des croissants* et *des pains au chocolat*.

Et comme boisson?

Il y a *du chocolat chaud*.

B Vous désirez?
   ou
   Qu'est-ce que vous prenez?

Un croissant, s'il vous plaît.

C Vous avez *soif*, vous voulez *du thé*?

Ah oui, j'ai *soif*, je prends *du thé*.

Regardez maintenant: les fiches B1 et B2

Unité neuf — cent trois — 103

Parlons

Série Deux

1. Qu'est-ce que vous faites ici?
2. Nous jouons au football.
3. Vous jouez très bien, je crois.
4. Oui, nous jouons assez bien.

Pour utiliser chaque expression avec chaque photo, changez les mots en italique.

A Qu'est-ce que *vous faites* ici?	B *Vous travaillez* très bien, je crois.
On mange.	Ah, oui, *nous travaillons* assez bien.

C J'aime *chanter*, moi.
Vous chantez très bien, *madame*.

Regardez maintenant: les fiches C1, C2 et C3

104 cent quatre

Unité neuf

Parlons... avec un(e) partenaire

Moi, je suis **A**. Toi, tu es **B**.

D'accord.

| A | Bonjour, | mademoiselle.
madame.
monsieur. | Qu'est-ce que vous | désirez?
prenez? |

| B | Bonjour, | madame.
monsieur. | Je voudrais | des croissants,
du pain avec de la confiture,
un croissant, | s'il vous plaît. |

| A | Bien, | mademoiselle.
madame.
monsieur. | Et comme boisson, il y a | du thé, du café au lait,
du chocolat chaud
ou du jus d'orange. |

| B | Un | thé,
café au lait,
jus d'orange,
chocolat chaud, | s'il vous plaît. |

| A | C'est tout? | | B | Oui, | madame.
monsieur. | C'est tout. |

* * * * * *

| B | C'est combien,
Ça fait combien, | s'il vous plaît? |

| A | Alors, ça fait | 15
21
32 | francs, s'il vous plaît, | mademoiselle.
madame.
monsieur. |

| B | 15
21
32 | francs. Voilà, | madame.
monsieur. |

| A | Très bien.
Parfait.
Merci. |

Regardez maintenant: la fiche D1

Unité neuf   cent cinq 105

Parlons... en situation

LE PETIT DÉJEUNER AU CAFÉ

Why not organise your own French **petit déjeuner** at school. Plan the event carefully so that the food is as French as possible. For example, make sure that the bread is **une baguette** - a French stick. You might even find a baker's or a supermarket that sells **croissants**. Don't forget to make a sign with a French name for your café. It will probably work well if you let the teacher act as the owner. You can pretend that the waiter or waitress is an adult too, which means that you will have to use **vous** with one another. Of course, anyone caught speaking English has to go hungry! **Bon appétit!**

By the way, if you want to know how to ask for the bill, look at page 109.

Regardez maintenant: les fiches E1 et E2

Ça c'est le français

1 VOUS DÉSIREZ?

When you go into a shop or a restaurant in France, the person serving you may ask:

Qu'est-ce que vous désirez?
(or just: **Vous désirez?**)

The commonest ways to begin your answer are to say:

Je voudrais... I'd like...
or
Je prends... I'll have...

2 VOUS

The French words for you we have been using so far are **tu** and **toi**. Use these with people your own age, members of your family, and animals.

Another very common way of saying you is **vous**. Use it:

a) when you are speaking to adults (unless they are part of your family).

e.g. **Monsieur Dumas, vous êtes très gentil.**
Mr Dumas, you are very kind.
Ah, bonjour, mademoiselle. Vous désirez?
Good morning, miss. What would you like?

b) when you are speaking to more than one person.

e.g. **Paul et Odette, vous avez faim ce matin?**
Paul and Odette, are you hungry this morning?
Salut, les gars! Qu'est-ce que vous faites ici?
Hi, you guys! What are you doing here?

3 NOUS

Even though **on** is often used to mean we, you also need to know and be able to use **nous**. Notice that the **nous** form of the verb almost always ends in **-ons**.

Demain nous allons manger des croissants au petit déjeuner.
Tomorrow we are going to eat croissants for breakfast.
Nous avons faim, bien sûr.
We're hungry, of course.

BUT NOTE:
Nous sommes désolé(e)s.
We're sorry.

4 VERBS

The table below shows you what you have learned so far about the Present Tense.

	Parler* (to speak)	Être (to be)	Avoir (to have)	Aller (to go)	Faire (to do)
je, j'	parle	suis	ai	vais	fais
tu	parles	es	as	vas	fais
il, elle	parle	est	a	va	fait
nous	parlons	sommes	avons	allons	faisons
vous	parlez	êtes	avez	allez	faites
ils, elles	parlent	sont	ont	vont	font

* **Parler** is just one example of the many regular **-er** verbs you have met so far.

Regardez maintenant: les fiches F1 et F2

Unité neuf

Baguettes, croissants et crêpes

Tu aimes le bon pain? French bread is so delicious and famous that British bakers call bread-sticks 'French' bread. The French call a loaf this shape **une baguette.**
Look up **baguette** in a French-English dictionary and you'll see that it has several other meanings as well as what you buy at **la boulangerie**.

Other things you might buy at the **boulangerie** include **un croissant; une brioche** - a cakey kind of bun; and **un pain au chocolat**, like a croissant but with bits of chocolate in it. **Mmm, c'est bon!**

You can often buy these things at **la pâtisserie** as well - together with a selection of **quiches** and a whole range of delicious, fattening **gâteaux**.

We've just seen some examples of words English has borrowed from French. Sometimes it's the other way round.. When you ask for **un sandwich** in France, you will get a section of **baguette** cut off and split down the middle. It may be buttered, but not always. And the filling? It might be **au jambon** - ham, **au fromage** - cheese, or **au pâté**. **Miam miam!**

Une crêpe is a pancake, either savoury or sweet. You might like to try one **au chocolat -** with chocolate filling. Or perhaps you'd prefer it **à la confiture de framboises** - with raspberry jam.

You can either buy **crêpes** at a street stall like the one on the left, or go into a **crêperie**, which is a restaurant that specialises in cooking them.

> Voilà, mademoiselle, une crêpe au jambon.

> Merci beaucoup.

Regardez maintenant: les fiches G1 et G2

cent huit

Unité neuf

Ça fait combien?

Once you've finished eating and drinking in a **café** or **restaurant** you have to think about paying for what you had. **L'addition** is the bill and **Ça fait combien?** means something like <u>How much will that be?</u> To be really polite you should add **s'il vous plaît**.

Another thing to check is whether the service charge or tip is included in the price you see on the menu. Sometimes you will see the words **service compris** - <u>service included</u> - printed at the bottom of a menu; or service will be added to a bill above the total. Otherwise you can ask, **Le service est compris?** If it isn't included, you should pay about 15% more than the total price.

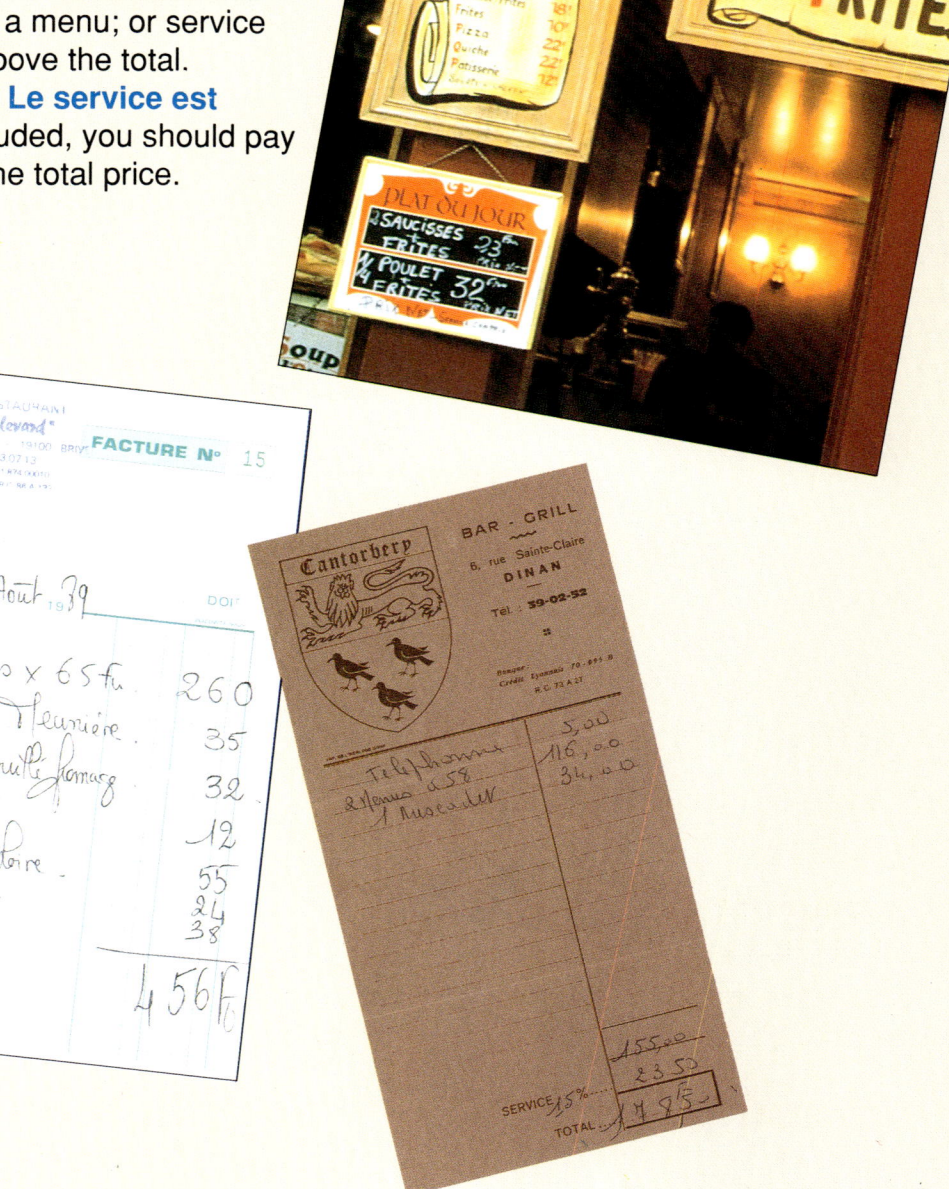

Regardez maintenant: la fiche H1

Unité neuf

Learning about language

LET'S BE FLEXIBLE

You have probably worked out for yourself by now that when you are studying another language you have to be very flexible. It's no use expecting every language to work in exactly the same way; anyone who speaks more than one language will tell you that often two languages can express the same idea quite differently.

You must have discovered already that the word-for-word approach doesn't get you very far at all. In most cases it's better to aim to understand groups of words or complete phrases.

In this unit, we have met the expression **Vous désirez?** Literally (that is, word-for-word), it means You desire? but the real English equivalent would be Yes, please? or Can I help you? or any other expression that people serving you might use. Look at this dictionary extract for the verb **désirer** and you will see that it is translated in many different ways, depending upon the situation.

désirer [deziRe]; *désirer faire quelque chose* to want or wish to do something; *que désirez-vous? (au magasin)* what would you like?; *(dans un bureau)* what can I do for you?; *Madame désire?* can I help you, Madam? *(dans un hotel)* you rang, Madam?

You can see that it often wouldn't do to choose the first translation in the list. You have to look at them all and then decide which one best fits the situation.

Regardez maintenant: la fiche I1

Leçon • Les sons • *Leçon* • Les sons • *Leçon*

Remember that as a foreign language student you have to become a good mimic. In other words you have to listen carefully to your pronunciation models (the tapes, your teacher, French people you might hear) and practise until you can imitate them well.

This is particularly important for the French nasal sounds - sounds you make through your nose. One common nasal sound occurs in the words and expressions below:

**Demain matin
J'ai faim.
J'aime bien le pain.**

If you're having trouble saying **pain** properly, try pronouncing p<u>an</u> through your nose, without letting your tongue touch the roof of your mouth.

Practise with these as well:

**Le terrain de tennis
Viens ici, mon petit chien.
Lucien, Justin et Alain sont tous des pingouins.**

Vocabulaire

C'EST BIEN LE MOT!

l'année scolaire(f)	school year
avoir faim	to be hungry
avoir soif	to be thirsty
avoir peur	to be afraid
la boulangerie	bakery
Cendrillon	Cinderella
la crêperie	pancake shop
délicieux, délicieuse	delicious
la fin	the end
gentil(le)	kind, nice
mauvais	bad
organiser	to organise
la pâtisserie	cake shop
pauvre	poor
presque	almost
sans	without
les vacances(f)	holidays

LE PETIT DÉJEUNER

la baguette	French loaf
le beurre	butter
le café	(black) coffee
le café au lait	white coffee
le chocolat chaud	hot chocolate
la confiture	jam
le pain	bread
le thé	tea

EXPRESSIONS UTILES

à l'année prochaine!	see you next year!
bon appétit!	enjoy your meal!
miam miam!	yum yum!
parfait!	perfect!
quelle barbe!	boring!
je voudrais...	I'd like...

AU RESTAURANT

la boisson	drink
le cheeseburger	cheeseburger
la crêpe	pancake
le fromage	cheese
le hamburger	hamburger
le jambon	ham
le jus d'orange	orange juice
en plein air	outside
au régime	on a diet
la sauce	sauce
la viande	meat

Quel progrès!

Félicitations! You are now able to use your French to do the following things:

- talk about food
- say you're hungry and thirsty
- order something to eat and drink
- ask for the bill
- pay the bill
- speak more formally in French

À l'année prochaine!

Regardez maintenant: les fiches I1, I2 et I3

Unité neuf

Appendice

Les pays et les continents

Afrique (f) ⎯ Africa
Algérie (f) ⎯ Algeria
Allemagne (f) ⎯ Germany
Amérique (f) ⎯ America
Angleterre (f) ⎯ England
Antilles (f) ⎯ West Indies
Asie (f) ⎯ Asia
Australie (f) ⎯ Australia
Belgique (f) ⎯ Belgium
Cambodge (m) ⎯ Cambodia
Canada (m) ⎯ Canada
Chine (f) ⎯ China
Espagne (f) ⎯ Spain
Europe (f) ⎯ Europe
Écosse (f) ⎯ Scotland
Égypte (f) ⎯ Egypt
France (f) ⎯ France
Grande-Bretagne (f) ⎯ Britain
Grèce (f) ⎯ Greece
Hollande (f) ⎯ Holland
Île Maurice (f) ⎯ Mauritius
Inde (f) ⎯ India
Irlande du Nord (f) ⎯ Northern Ireland
Irlande (f) ⎯ Republic of Ireland
Italie (f) ⎯ Italy
Japon (m) ⎯ Japan
Kenya (m) ⎯ Kenya
Maroc (m) ⎯ Morocco
Nouvelle Calédonie (f) ⎯ New Caledonia
Pakistan (m) ⎯ Pakistan
Portugal (m) ⎯ Portugal
Suisse (f) ⎯ Switzerland
Thaïlande (f) ⎯ Thailand
Tunisie (f) ⎯ Tunisia
Turquie (f) ⎯ Turkey

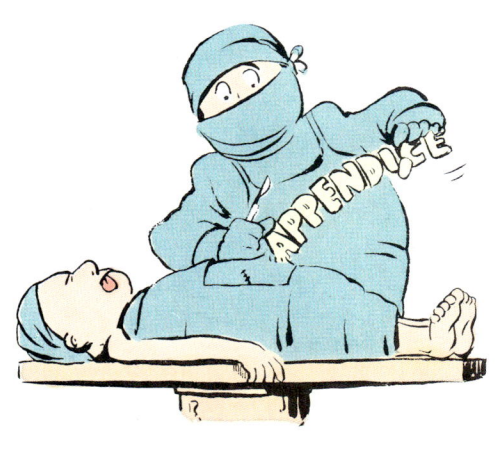

Les jours de la semaine

lundi ⎯ Monday
mardi ⎯ Tuesday
mercredi ⎯ Wednesday
jeudi ⎯ Thursday
vendredi ⎯ Friday
samedi ⎯ Saturday
dimanche ⎯ Sunday

Les mois

janvier ⎯ January
février ⎯ February
mars ⎯ March
avril ⎯ April
mai ⎯ May
juin ⎯ June
juillet ⎯ July
août ⎯ August
septembre ⎯ September
octobre ⎯ October
novembre ⎯ November
décembre ⎯ December

Les saisons

printemps (m) ⎯ spring
été (m) ⎯ summer
automne (m) ⎯ autumn
hiver (m) ⎯ winter

Les couleurs

blanc, blanche ⎯ white
bleu, bleue ⎯ blue
brun, brune ⎯ brown
gris, grise ⎯ grey
jaune ⎯ yellow
noir, noire ⎯ black
orange ⎯ orange
rose ⎯ pink
rouge ⎯ red
vert, verte ⎯ green
violet, violette ⎯ purple

Les chiffres

1 ⎯ un
2 ⎯ deux
3 ⎯ trois
4 ⎯ quatre
5 ⎯ cinq
6 ⎯ six
7 ⎯ sept
8 ⎯ huit
9 ⎯ neuf
10 ⎯ dix
11 ⎯ onze
12 ⎯ douze
13 ⎯ treize
14 ⎯ quatorze
15 ⎯ quinze
16 ⎯ seize
17 ⎯ dix-sept
18 ⎯ dix-huit
19 ⎯ dix-neuf
20 ⎯ vingt
21 ⎯ vingt et un
22 ⎯ vingt-deux
30 ⎯ trente
31 ⎯ trente et un
40 ⎯ quarante
50 ⎯ cinquante
60 ⎯ soixante
70 ⎯ soixante-dix
71 ⎯ soixante et onze
72 ⎯ soixante-douze
80 ⎯ quatre-vingts
81 ⎯ quatre-vingt-un
82 ⎯ quatre-vingt-deux
90 ⎯ quatre-vingt-dix
99 ⎯ quatre-vingt-dix-neuf
100 ⎯ cent
101 ⎯ cent un
200 ⎯ deux cents
201 ⎯ deux cent un
1000 ⎯ mille

Vocabulaire français-anglais

A

à — to, at, in
à bas — down with
à bientôt — see you soon
à demain — see you tomorrow
à table — at table; to the table
accident (m) — accident
addition (f) — bill
adorer — to love
âge (m) — age
aider — to help
aimer — to love, like
album (m)
  de famille — family album
aller — to go
allez-y! — go ahead!
allô! — hello! (when answering the telephone)
alors — then, well
ami (m),
amie (f) — friend
amour (m) — love
an (m) — year
  j'ai douze ans — I am twelve years old
anglais,
anglaise — English
année (f) — year
année scolaire — school year
août (m) — August
appartement (m) — apartment, flat
appelle:
  je m'appelle — my name is
  tu t'appelles — your name is
appétit (m) — appetite
après — after
après-midi (m,f) — afternoon
argent (m) — money
arriver — to arrive
asseyez-vous! — sit down!
assez — enough, sufficient
assieds-toi! — sit down!
atlantique — Atlantic
atmosphère (f) — atmosphere
attendre — to wait
attention! — pay attention!
au revoir — goodbye
au téléphone — on the telephone
aujourd'hui — today
aussi — also
automne (m) — autumn
autoroute (f) — motorway
avec — with
avion (m) — plane
avril (m) — April

B

babyfoot (m) — table football
baguette (f) — French loaf of bread
basket (m) — basketball; training shoe
bateau (m) — boat, ship
bateau-mouche (m) — pleasure-boat

beau, belle — handsome, beautiful
beaucoup — a lot of
bébé (m) — baby
bête — stupid
beurk! — yuk!
beurre (m) — butter
bien — well, good
bien sûr — of course
bientôt — soon
bienvenue — welcome
blanc, blanche — white
bleu, bleue — blue
blond, blonde — blond
boisson (f) — drink
bon, bonne — good
  bon appétit! — enjoy your meal!
  bon courage! — good luck!
  bon voyage! — have a good journey!
  bonne chance! — good luck!
  bonne fête! — happy name day!
  bonne nuit — good night
bonbon (m) — sweet
bonjour — good day, hello
bonsoir — good evening
bouche (f) — mouth
boulangerie (f) — bakery
boutique (f) — shop
bras (m) — arm
bravo! — well done!
brioche (f) — bun
britannique — British
brochure (f) — brochure
brun, brune — brown
bureau (m) — office

C

ça — this, that
ça alors! — you don't say!
ça bouge! — things are really moving!
ça suffit! — that's enough!
ça va? — how are you?
ça va — things are OK; that's all right; that's enough
  ça va bien — things are going well
  ça va mal — things are going badly
  ça va très bien — I'm very well
cadeau (m) — present, gift
café (m) — coffee; café
cahier (m) — exercise book
calendrier (m) — calendar
calme — calm, quiet
cartable (m) — school-bag, satchel
carte (f) — map
casse-cou (m) — daredevil
casse-pieds (m) — nuisance, pain in the neck
catastrophe (f) — disaster, catastrophe
  quelle catastrophe! — what a disaster!

cathédrale (f) — cathedral
ce, cet, cette — this, that
c'est — it is; this is; that is
  c'est qui? — who is it?
Cendrillon — Cinderella
centimètre (m) — centimetre
chaîne stéréo (f) — stereo
chambre (f) — bedroom
champion (m),
championne (f) — champion
chance:
  bonne chance — good luck
changer — to change
chanson (f) — song
chanter — to sing
chaque — each, every
chat (m)
chatte (f) — cat
château (m) — stately home, castle
chaud, chaude — hot
  il fait chaud — it's hot
chauffeur (m) — driver, chauffeur
chaumière (f) — cottage
chercher — to look for
cheval (m) — horse
cheveux (m pl) — hair
chez moi — at my place
chez toi — at your place
chien (m),
  chienne (f) — dog
chiffre (m) — number
chocolat (m) — chocolate
chouchou (m) — teacher's-pet
chouette! — great! smashing!
ciel (m) — sky
cinéma (m) — cinema
cinq — five
cinquante — fifty
classe (f) — class
classique — classical
coeur (m) — heart
combien de? — how much? how many?
comédie
  musicale (f) — musical
comme — as, like
commencer — to begin
comment? — how?
  comment ça va — how are you? how are things going?
  comment s'appelle-t-il? — what's his name
comprendre — to understand
compter — to count
concours (m) — competition
concurrent (m),
  concurrente (f) — competitor
confiture (f) — jam
connaître — to know
content,
  contente — happy, pleased
continent (m) — continent
corps (m) — body
couleur (f) — colour
coupe (f) — cup, trophy
courses (f pl) — shopping
côte (f) — coast

Vocabulaire   cent treize 113

crayon (m) _____ pencil
crème (f)
 solaire _____ sun cream
crêpe (f) _____ pancake
crêperie (f) _____ pancake shop
croire _____ to believe
croissant (m) _ croissant
cuisine (f) _____ kitchen; cooking

D

d'accord _____ all right
dame (f) _____ lady
dans _____ in
danse (f) _____ dancing
danser _____ to dance
de _____ of
dé (m) _____ dice
décembre (m) _ December
défense
 plongerx _____ no diving
déjeuner _____ lunch
délicieux,
 délicieuse _____ delicious
demain _____ tomorrow
désirer _____ to want
dernier,
 dernière _____ last
des _____ some; of the
description (f) _ description
désolé,
 désolée _____ sorry
dessin (m) _____ drawing
détester _____ to hate, detest
deux _____ two
devoirs (m pl) _____ homework
Dieu _____ God
différent,
 différente _____ different
difficile _____ difficult
dimanche (m) _ Sunday
dire _____ to say
directeur (m),
 directrice (f) _ head teacher
dis donc _____ tell me
dix _____ ten
donc _____ so, therefore
doucement _____ slowly
douze _____ twelve
du _____ some; of the

E

école (f) _____ school
écouter _____ to listen (to)
éducation (f)
 physique _____ physical education
égaler _____ to be equal to
église (f) _____ church
élégant,
 élégante _____ elegant
elle _____ she
émission de
 télévision (f) _____ television programme
en _____ in
 en forme _____ on form
 en retard _____ late
enfant (m, f) _____ child

114 cent quatorze

énorme _____ enormous
ensemble _____ together
entre _____ between
entrer _____ to enter
 avoir **envie** de _ to want
équipe (f) _____ team
équitation (f) _ riding
été (m) _____ summer
être _____ to be
étudiant (m),
 étudiante (f) _ student
excusez-moi _ excuse me
expression (f) _ expression
extra _____ special
extraordinaire _ extraordinary

F

faim (f) _____ hunger
 j'ai faim _____ I'm hungry
faire _____ to do; to make
famille (f) _____ family
fantastique _____ fantastic
fantôme (m) _____ phantom, ghost
femme (f) _____ woman
fenêtre (f) _____ window
fermer _____ to close, to shut
félicitations (f) _ congratulations
fête (f) _____ name day
 bonne **fête!** _ happy name day!
février (m) _____ February
fiche (f) _____ worksheet
fille (f) _____ girl; daughter
film (m) _____ film
fils (m) _____ son
fin (f) _____ !end, finish
forme (f) _____ form, shape
 en **forme** _____ on form, in shape
formidable _____ great, tremendous
fort, forte _____ strong
fou, folle _____ mad, crazy
fraise (f) _____ strawberry
framboise (f) _ raspberry
français,
 française _____ French
francophone _ French-speaking
franc (m) _____ franc
frère (m) _____ brother
froid, froide _ cold
 j'ai **froid** _____ I'm cold
fromage (m) _____ cheese
frontière (f) _____ frontier
funiculaire (m) _ funicular railway
futur (m) _____ future

G

gagner _____ to earn; to win
garçon (m) _____ boy
gare (f) _____ station
gars (m) _____ lad
gâteau (m) _____ cake
gentil, gentille _ kind, nice
geler _____ to freeze
géographie (f) _ geography
gomme (f) _____ rubber
grand, grande _ big, large
gris, grise _____ grey
groupe (m) _____ group

H

habiter _____ to live in, at
hein? _____ what?
heure (f) _____ hour
histoire (f) _____ history
hiver (m) _____ winter
honnête _____ honest
huit _____ eight

I

ici _____ here
idéal, idéale _ ideal
idée (f) _____ idea
il _____ he
il y a _____ there is, there are
île (f) _____ island
impossible _____ impossible
intelligent,
 intelligente _____ clever, intelligent
intéressant,
 intéressante _ interesting
italique:
 en **italique** _____ in italic

J

jambe (f) _____ leg
jambon (m) _____ ham
janvier (m) _____ January
jardin (m) _____ garden
jaune _____ yellow
je _____ I
jeter _____ to throw
jeton (m) _____ counter
jeu (m) _____ game
jeux vidéo _____ video games
jeudi (m) _____ Thursday
jeune _____ young
joue (f) _____ cheek
jouer _____ to play
joueur (m) _____ player
jour (m) _____ day
journal (m) _____ newspaper
juillet (m) _____ July
juin (m) _____ June
jus (m) **d'orange** orange juice

K

kilomètre (m) _ kilometre

L

la, le, l', les _ the
là _____ there
lait (m) _____ milk
langue (f) _____ language, tongue
leçon (f) _____ lesson
lecture (f) _____ reading
 bonne **lecture!** good reading!
lendemain (m) _ the next day
lettre (f) _____ letter
lève-toi _____ stand, get up
levez-vous _ stand, get up
légendaire _____ legendary

Vocabulaire

librairie (f) — bookshop
libre — free
livre (m) — book
  livre de l'étudiant — student's book
lundi (m) — Monday

ma — my
madame, Mme — madam, Mrs, Ms
mademoiselle, Mlle — Miss
magasin (m) — shop, store
magnifique — magnificent
mai (m) — May
maillot (m) — football shirt
main (f) — hand
maintenant — now
mais — but
maison (f) — house
mal — bad, badly
maman (f) — mum
manche (f) — sleeve
manger — to eat
mardi (m) — Tuesday
mari (m) — husband
marotte (f) — life-size puppet
marrant, marrante — funny
mars (m) — March
maths (f) — Maths
matière (f) — subject
matin (m) — morning
mauvais, mauvaise — bad, faulty
mauve — mauve
méchant, méchante — naughty, bad
médiéval, médiévale — medieval
Méditerranée (f) — Mediterranean sea
ménage (m) — housework
menteur (m), **menteuse** (f) — liar
mer (f) — sea
merci — thank you
mercredi (m) — Wednesday
mère (f) — mother
mes — my
métro (m) — underground
miam-miam — yum-yum
miaou — miaow
mince! — drat!
minette (f) — puss, kitty
minute (f) — minute
misérable — wretched
moche — ugly
mode (f) — fashion
  à la **mode** — in fashion
moi — me
mois (m) — month
mon — my
monde (m) — world
monsieur, M — sir, Mr
montagne (f) — mountain
mot (m) — word
mouche (f) — fly
musclé, musclée — muscular
musée (m) — museum
musique (f) — music

N

nager — to swim
natation (f) — swimming
né, née — born
ne pas — not
neiger — to snow
neuf — nine
nez (m) — nose
niveau (m) — level
noir, noire — black
nom (m) — name
non — no
nord — north
normal, normale — normal
nos — our
notre — our
nous — we
nouveau, nouvelle — new
novembre (m) — November
nuit (f) — night
numéro (m) — number

O

océan (m) — ocean
octobre (m) — October
oeil (m) — eye
oeuf (m) — egg
ohé! — hey there!
oiseau (m) — bird
onze — eleven
orange — orange
ordinateur (m) — computer
oreille (f) — ear
organiser — to organize
original, originale — original
ou — or
où? — where?
ouah — woof
oublier — to forget
ouf! — whew!
oui — yes
ouvert, ouverte — open
ouvrir — to open

P

page (f) — page
pain (m) — bread
palais (m) — palace
papa (m) — dad, father
papeterie (f) — stationer
papier (m) — paper
par — by
parapluie (m) — umbrella
parasol (m) — parasol
parce que — because
pardon — pardon
parfait, parfaite — perfect
parler — to talk
partenaire (m,f) — partner
partie (f) — part
partir — to go, to leave
partout — everywhere

pas:
  pas mal — not bad
  pas mauvais — not bad
  pas grand-chose — not much
passer — to pass; to call by
pâté (m) — pâté
pâtisserie (f) — cake shop
pauvre — poor
pays (m) — country
pendant — during
pension (f) — boarding-house
péniche (f) — barge
père (m) — father
personne (f) — person
petit, petite — little; small
petit déjeuner (m) — breakfast
peu:
  un **peu** — a little, a few
peur:
  j'ai **peur** — I'm afraid
peut-être — perhaps
photo (f) — photo
pied (m) — foot
pingouin (m) — penguin
pique-nique (m) — picnic
piscine (f) — swimming pool
place (f) — seat
planche (f) à **roulettes** — skateboard
plein, pleine — full
pleuvoir — to rain
plonger — to dive
pluriel (m) — plural
poème (m) — poem
poisson (m) — fish
pont (m) — bridge
porte (f) — door
porter — to carry
possible — possible
pour — for
pour cent — per cent
pourquoi — why
premier, première — first
prendre — to take
presque — almost
presse (f) — press
préféré, préférée — favourite
préférer — to prefer
prénom (m) — first name
préparer — to prepare
président (m) — president
printemps (m) — spring
prix (m) — price
prochain, prochaine — next
professeur (m,f) — teacher
progrès (m) — progress
puis — then

Q

quand — when
quarante — forty
quatorze — fourteen
quatre — four
quatre-vingts — eighty
que — that

quel? quelle? — what?, which?
  quel âge as-tu? how old are you?
  quelle page? — what page?
  quelle barbe! — what a drag!
quelque chose — something
quelqu'un,
  quelqu'une — someone, somebody
qu'est-ce que? — what?
qui — who
quinze — fifteen

R

radio (f) — radio
raison (f) — reason
rare — rare
réel, réelle — real
regarder — to look (at)
régime (m) — diet
règle (f) — ruler
regretter — to regret
rendez-vous (m) — meeting, date
rentrer — to go/come home
répétition (f) — rehearsal
république (f) — republic
restaurant (m) — restaurant
rester — to stay
résultat (m) — result
retard:
  en **retard** — late
retour (m) — return
retourner — to return
revoir:
  au **revoir** — goodbye
riche — rich
rivière (f) — river
rose — pink
rouge — red
route (f) — road
rue (f) — street

S

sa — his, her
sacré, sacrée — sacred
saison (f) — season
sais: je **sais** — I know
  je ne **sais** pas — I don't know
salle (f) — room
salle de classe — classroom
salle de jeux — amusement arcade
salut! — hello, hi
salutations (f) — greetings
samedi (m) — Saturday
sandwich (m) — sandwich
sans — without
sauce (f) — sauce
savoir — to know
sciences (f pl) — science
seize — sixteen
semaine (f) — week
sept — seven
septembre (m) — September
série (f) — series
service (m) — service, tip
ses — his, her

seul, seule — alone
seulement — only
sévère — severe
si — if
silence! — silence!
singulier:
  au **singulier** — in the singular
situation (f) — situation
six — six
soeur (f) — sister
soif: j'ai **soif** — I'm thirsty
soir (m) — night, evening
soixante — sixty
soleil (m) — sun
son — his, her
sondage (m) — survey
sourire (m) — smile
spectacle (m) — sight, spectacle
spectateur (m) — spectator
spécial,
  spéciale — special
sport (m) — sport
sportif,
  sportive — athletic
stéréo (f) — stereo
style (m) — style
stylo (m) — pen
sud — south
suffit: ça **suffit** — that's enough
super — great
supplémentaire — extra
sur — on
sûr, sûre — sure, contain
  bien **sûr** — of course; sure!
surligneur (m) — highlighter
surprise (f) — surprise
sympa — nice, friendly

T

ta — your
table (f) — table
tais-toi! — be quiet!
taisez-vous! — be quiet!
télé (f) — TV
téléphone (m) — telephone
télévision (f) — television
temps (m) — weather
tennis (m) — tennis
terrain (m) de
  tennis — tennis court
tes — your
test (m) — test
tête (f) — head
thé (m) — tea
théâtre (m) — theatre
toc toc! — knock! knock!
toi — you
ton — your
toucher — to touch
toujours — always
tour (f) — tower
tour (m) — trip; circuit
tous, tout,
  toute — all
travailler — to work
treize — thirteen

trente — thirty
très — very
trois — three
trop — too
trousse (f) — pencil-case
t-shirt (m) — T-shirt
tu — you
tunnel (m) — tunnel

U

un, une — a, an, one
unité (f) — unit
usine (f) — factory
utile — useful
utiliser — to use

V

vacances (f pl) — holidays
vaisselle (f) — washing up
  faire la
  vaisselle — to do the washing up
valable — valid
vas-y! — go ahead!
vedette (f) — star (of film, sport)
vendredi (m) — Friday
venir — to come
vent (m) — wind
ventre (m) — stomach; belly
vert, verte — green
vélo (m) — bike
viande (f) — meat
vidéo (f) — video
vie (f) — life
ville (f) — town
vingt — twenty
violet, violette — purple, violet
visage (m) — face
visiter — to visit
vite — quick
vivre — to live
vocabulaire (m) — vocabulary
voici — here is
voilà — there (it) is
voir — to see
voisin (m),
  voisine (f) — neighbour
voiture (f) — car
votre — your
voudrais:
  je **voudrais** — I'd like
vouloir — to want, wish
vous — you
voyage (m) — journey, voyage
vrai, vraie — true
vraiment — really

W Y Z

week-end (m) — weekend
y — there
  il **y a** — there is, there are
yeux (m pl) — eyes
zut! — blast!

English-French Vocabulary

A

a, an	**un, une**
accident	**accident** (m)
I'm afraid	**j'ai peur**
after	**après**
afternoon	**après-midi** (m,f)
age	**âge** (m)
all	**tous, tout, toute**
all right	**d'accord**
almost	**presque**
alone	**seul, seule**
also	**aussi**
always	**toujours**
amusement arcade	**salle de jeux**
appetite	**appétit** (m)
April	**avril** (m)
arm	**bras** (m)
to arrive	**arriver**
at	**à**
athletic	**sportif, sportive**
Atlantic	**atlantique**
atmosphere	**atmosphère** (f)
pay attention!	**attention!**
August	**août** (m)
autumn	**automne** (m)

B

baby	**bébé** (m)
bad	**mauvais, mauvaise**
not bad	**pas mal**
badly	**mal**
bakery	**boulangerie** (f)
barge	**péniche** (f)
basketball	**basket** (m)
to be	**être**
to be equal to	**égaler**
beautiful	**beau, belle**
because	**parce que**
bedroom	**chambre** (f)
to begin	**commencer**
to believe	**croire**
between	**entre**
big	**grand, grande**
bike	**vélo** (m)
bill	**addition** (f)
bird	**oiseau** (m)
black	**noir, noire**
blast	**zut!**
blond	**blond, blonde**
blue	**bleu, bleue**
boarding-house	**pension** (f)
boat, ship	**bateau** (m)
body	**corps** (m)
book	**livre** (m)
student's book	**livre de l'étudiant**
bookshop	**librairie** (f)
born	**né, née**
boy	**garçon** (m)
bread	**pain** (m)
breakfast	**petit déjeuner** (m)
bridge	**pont** (m)
British	**britannique**
brochure	**brochure** (f)
brother	**frère** (m)
brown	**brun, brune**
bun	**brioche** (f)
but	**mais**
butter	**beurre** (m)
by	**par**

C

café	**café** (m)
cake	**gâteau** (m)
cake shop	**pâtisserie** (f)
calendar	**calendrier** (m)
to call by	**passer**
calm	**calme**
car	**voiture** (f)
to carry	**porter**
castle	**château** (m)
cat	**chat** (m) **chatte** (f)
cathedral	**cathédrale** (f)
centimetre	**centimètre** (m)
champion	**champion** (m) **championne** (f)
to change	**changer**
cheek	**joue** (f)
cheese	**fromage** (m)
child	**enfant** (m, f)
chocolate	**chocolat** (m)
church	**église** (f)
Cinderella	**Cendrillon**
cinema	**cinéma** (m)
circuit	**tour** (m)
class	**classe** (f)
classical	**classique**
classroom	**salle de classe**
clever	**intelligent, intelligente**
to close	**fermer**
coast	**côte** (f)
coffee	**café** (m)
cold	**froid, froide**
I'm cold	**j'ai froid**
colour	**couleur** (f)
to come	**venir**
competition	**concours** (m)
competitor	**concurrent** (m), **concurrente** (f)
computer	**ordinateur** (m)
congratulations	**félicitations** (f)
continent	**continent** (m)
cooking	**cuisine** (f)
cottage	**chaumière** (f)
to count	**compter**
counter	**jeton** (m)
country	**pays** (m)
of course	**bien sûr**
croissant	**croissant** (m)
cup, trophy	**coupe** (f)

D

dad	**papa** (m)
to dance	**danser**
dancing	**danse** (f)
daredevil	**casse-cou** (m)
daughter	**fille** (f)
day	**jour** (m)
December	**décembre** (m)
delicious	**délicieux, délicieuse**
description	**description** (f)
dice	**dé** (m)
diet	**régime** (m)
different	**différent, différente**
difficult	**difficile**
disaster	**catastrophe** (f)
what a disaster!	**quelle catastrophe!**
to dive	**plonger**
diving	**défense de plonger**
to do	**faire**
dog	**chien** (m), **chienne** (f)
door	**porte** (f)
down with	**à bas**
what a drag!	**quelle barbe!**
drat!	**mince!**
drawing	**dessin** (m)
drink	**boisson** (f)
driver	**chauffeur** (m)
during	**pendant**

E

each	**chaque**
ear	**oreille** (f)
to earn	**gagner**
to eat	**manger**
egg	**oeuf** (m)
eight	**huit**
eighty	**quatre-vingts**
elegant	**élégant, élégante**
eleven	**onze**
end, finish	**fin** (f)
English	**anglais, anglaise**
enjoy your meal!	**bon appétit!**
enormous	**énorme**
enough, sufficient	**assez**
that's enough!	**ça suffit!**
to enter	**entrer**
evening	**soir** (m)
everywhere	**partout**
excuse me	**excusez-moi**
exercise book	**cahier** (m)
expression	**expression** (f)
extra	**supplémentaire**
extraordinary	**extraordinaire**
eye	**oeil** (m)
eyes	**yeux** (m pl)

F

face	**visage** (m)
factory	**usine** (f)
family	**famille** (f)
family album	**album** (m) **de famille**

Vocabulaire   cent dix-sept   117

fantastic	fantastique
fashion	mode (f)
in fashion	à la mode
father	père (m)
favourite	préféré, préférée
February	février (m)
a few	un peu
fifteen	quinze
fifty	cinquante
film	film (m)
first	premier, première
first name	prénom (m)
fish	poisson (m)
five	cinq
to flat	appartement (m)
fly	mouche (f)
foot	pied (m)
football shirt	maillot (m)
for	pour
to forget	oublier
on form	en forme
forty	quarante
four	quatre
fourteen	quatorze
franc	franc (m)
free	libre
to freeze	geler
French	français, française
French-speaking	francophone
Friday	vendredi (m)
friend	ami (m), amie (f)
frontier	frontière (f)
full	plein, pleine
funicular railway	funiculaire (m)
funny	marrant, marrante
future	futur (m)

G

game	jeu (m)
garden	jardin (m)
geography	géographie (f)
ghost	fantôme (m)
girl	fille (f)
to go	aller
go ahead!	allez-y!, vas-y!
God	Dieu
good!	bien!
good	bon, bonne
good day	bonjour
good evening	bonsoir
have a good journey!	bon voyage!
good luck!	bonne chance! bon courage!
good night	bonne nuit
goodbye	au revoir
great	formidable, super, chouette
green	vert, verte
greetings	salutations (f pl)
grey	gris, grise
group	groupe (m)

H

hair	cheveux (m pl)
ham	jambon (m)
hand	main (f)
handsome	beau
happy	content, contente
happy name day!	bonne fête!
hate	détester
he	il
head	tête (f)
head teacher	directeur (m), directrice (f)
heart	coeur (m)
hello	bonjour, salut
hello! (when answering telephone)	allô!
to help	aider
her	son, sa, ses
here	ici
here is	voici
hey there!	ohé!
highlighter	surligneur (m)
his	son, sa, ses
history	histoire (f)
holidays	vacances (f pl)
to come, go home	rentrer
homework	devoirs (m pl)
honest	honnête
horse	cheval (m)
horses	chevaux (m pl)
hot	chaud, chaude
it's hot	il fait chaud
hour	heure (f)
house	maison (f)
housework	ménage (m)
how?	comment?
how are you?	ça va?
how are things going?	comment ça va?
how much? how many?	combien de?
hunger	faim (f)
hungry	j'ai faim
husband	mari (m)

I

I	je
idea	idée (f)
ideal	idéal, idéale
if	si
impossible	impossible
in	à, dans, en
interesting	intéressant, intéressante
island	île (f)
it is	c'est
in italics	en italique

J

jam	confiture (f)
January	janvier (m)
journey, voyage	voyage (m)
July	juillet (m)
June	juin (m)

K

kilometre	kilomètre (m)
kind	gentil, gentille
kitchen	cuisine (f)
knock! knock!	toc toc!
to know	connaître, savoir
I do not know	je ne sais pas
I know	je sais

L

lad	gars (m)
lady	dame (f)
language	langue (f)
large	grand, grande
last	dernier, dernière
late	en retard
to leave	partir
leg	jambe (f)
legendary	légendaire
lesson	leçon (f)
letter	lettre (f)
level	niveau
liar	menteur (m), menteuse (f)
life	vie (f)
like	comme
I'd like	je voudrais
to listen (to)	écouter
little	petit, petite
a little	un peu
to live	vivre
to live in, at	habiter
French loaf	baguette (f)
to look for	chercher
to look (at)	regarder
a lot of	beaucoup
love	amour (m)
to love	adorer, aimer
lunch	déjeuner

M

mad	fou, folle
madam	madame, Mme
magnificent	magnifique
to make	faire
map	carte (f)
March	mars (m)
Maths	maths (f)
mauve	mauve
May	mai (m)
me	moi
meat	viande (f)
medieval	médiéval, médiévale
Mediterranean sea	Méditerranée (f)
meeting, date	rendez-vous (m)
miaow	miaou
milk	lait (m)
minute	minute (f)
Miss	mademoiselle, Mlle
Monday	lundi (m)
money	argent (m)
month	mois (m)
morning	matin (m)
mother	mère (f)
motorway	autoroute (f)
mountain	montagne (f)
mouth	bouche (f)
Mr	monsieur
Mrs, Ms	madame, Mme

mum	**maman** (f)
muscular	**musclé, musclée**
museum	**musée** (m)
music	**musique** (f)
musical	**comédie musicale** (f)
my	**mon, ma, mes**

N

name	**nom** (m)
my name is	**je m'appelle**
your name is	**tu t'appelles**
what's his name?	**comment s'appelle-t-il?**
name day	**fête** (f)
happy name day!	**bonne fête!**
naughty	**méchant, méchante**
neighbour	**voisin** (m), **voisine** (f)
new	**nouveau, nouvelle**
newspaper	**journal** (m)
next	**prochain, prochaine**
next day	**lendemain** (m)
nice	**gentil, gentille; sympa**
night	**nuit** (f)
nine	**neuf**
no	**non**
normal	**normal, normale**
north	**nord**
nose	**nez** (m)
not	**ne pas**
not bad	**pas mal; pas mauvais**
not much	**pas grand-chose**
November	**novembre** (m)
now	**maintenant**
nuisance	**casse-pieds** (m)
number	**chiffre** (m); **numéro** (m)

O

ocean	**océan** (m)
October	**octobre** (m)
of	**de**
office	**bureau** (m)
how old are you?	**quel âge as-tu?**
on	**sur**
on form, in shape	**en forme**
one	**un**
only	**seulement**
open	**ouvert, ouverte**
to open	**ouvrir**
or	**ou**
orange	**orange**
orange juice	**jus** (m) **d'orange**
to organize	**organiser**
original	**original, originale**
our	**notre; nos**

P

page	**page** (f)
what page?	**quelle page?**
palace	**palais** (m)
pancake	**crêpe** (f)
pancake shop	**crêperie** (f)
paper	**papier** (m)
parasol	**parasol** (m)
part	**partie** (f)
partner	**partenaire** (m,f)
pâté	**pâté** (m)
pen	**stylo** (m)
pencil	**crayon** (m)
pencil-case	**trousse** (f)
penguin	**pingouin** (m)
per cent	**pour cent**
perfect	**parfait, parfaite**
perhaps	**peut-être**
person	**personne** (f)
photo	**photo** (f)
physical education	**éducation** (f) **physique**
picnic	**pique-nique** (m)
pink	**rose**
at my place	**chez moi**
at your place	**chez toi**
plane	**avion** (m)
to play	**jouer**
player	**joueur** (m)
pleasure-boat	**bateau-mouche** (m)
plural	**pluriel** (m)
poem	**poème** (m)
poor	**pauvre**
possible	**possible**
to prefer	**préférer**
to prepare	**préparer**
present	**cadeau** (m)
president	**président** (m)
press	**presse** (f)
price	**prix** (m)
programme	**émission de télévision** (f)
progress	**progrès** (m)
puppet	**marotte** (f)
purple	**violet, violette**
puss, kitty	**minette** (f)

Q

quick	**vite**
quiet!	**tais-toi!; taisez-vous!**

R

radio	**radio** (f)
to rain	**pleuvoir**
rare	**rare**
raspberry	**framboise** (f)
reading	**lecture** (f)
good reading!	**bonne lecture!**
real	**réel, réelle**
really	**vraiment**
reason	**raison** (f)
red	**rouge**
to regret	**regretter**
rehearsal	**répétition** (f)
republic	**république** (f)
restaurant	**restaurant** (m)
result	**résultat** (m)
return	**retour** (m)
to return	**retourner**
rich	**riche**
riding	**équitation** (f)
river	**rivière** (f)
road	**route** (f)
room	**salle** (f)
rubber	**gomme** (f)
ruler	**règle** (f)

S

sacred	**sacré, sacrée**
sandwich	**sandwich** (m)
Saturday	**samedi** (m)
sauce	**sauce** (f)
to say	**dire**
school	**école** (f)
school-bag	**cartable** (m)
science	**sciences** (f pl)
sea	**mer** (f)
season	**saison** (f)
seat	**place** (f)
to see	**voir**
see you soon	**à bientôt**
see you tomorrow	**à demain**
September	**septembre** (m)
series	**série** (f)
seven	**sept**
severe	**sévère**
shape	**forme** (f)
she	**elle**
shop	**boutique** (f); **magasin** (m)
shopping	**courses** (f pl)
to shut	**fermer**
sight	**spectacle** (m)
silence!	**silence!**
to sing	**chanter**
singular	**au singulier**
sir	**monsieur**
sister	**soeur** (f)
sit down!	**assieds-toi!; asseyez-vous!**
six	**six**
sixteen	**seize**
sixty	**soixante**
skateboard	**planche** (f) **à roulettes**
sky	**ciel** (m)
sleeve	**manche** (f)
slowly	**doucement**
small	**petit, petite**
smile	**sourire** (m)
to snow	**neiger**
so	**donc**
someone, somebody	**quelqu'un, quelqu'une**
something	**quelque chose**
some; of the	**du; des**
son	**fils** (m)
song	**chanson** (f)
soon	**bientôt**
sorry	**désolé, désolée; pardon!**
I'm sorry	**je suis désolé, je suis désolée**
south	**sud**
special	**extra**
special	**spécial, spéciale**
spectator	**spectateur** (m)
sport	**sport** (m)

spring	**printemps** (m)
stand up	**levez-vous**
stand up	**lève-toi**
star (of film, sport)	**vedette** (f)
station	**gare** (f)
stationer	**papeterie** (f)
to stay	**rester**
stereo	**chaîne stéréo** (f); **stéréo**
stomach	**ventre** (m)
store	**magasin** (m)
strawberry	**fraise** (f)
street	**rue** (f)
strong	**fort, forte**
student	**étudiant** (m), **étudiante** (f)
stupid	**bête**
style	**style** (m)
subject	**matière** (f)
summer	**été** (m)
sun	**soleil** (m)
sun cream	**crème** (f) **solaire**
Sunday	**dimanche** (m)
surprise	**surprise** (f)
survey	**sondage** (m)
sweet	**bonbon** (m)
to swim	**nager**
swimming	**natation** (f)
swimming pool	**piscine** (f)

T

table	**table** (f)
table football	**babyfoot** (m)
at table; to the table	**à table**
to take	**prendre**
to talk	**parler**
tea	**thé** (m)
teacher	**professeur** (m,f)
teacher's-pet	**chouchou** (m)
team	**équipe** (f)
telephone	**téléphone** (m)
on the telephone	**au téléphone**
television	**télévision** (f)
tell me	**dis donc**
ten	**dix**
tennis	**tennis** (m)
tennis court	**terrain** (m) **de tennis**
test	**test** (m)
thank you	**merci**
that	**que**
that is	**c'est**
that's all right	**ça va**
the	**la, le, l', les**
theatre	**théâtre** (m)
then	**alors; puis**
there	**là; y**
there (it) is	**voilà**
there is, there are	**il y a**
things are going badly	**ça va mal**
things are going well	**ça va bien**
things are really moving!	**ça bouge!**
I'm thirsty	**j'ai soif**
thirteen	**treize**
thirty	**trente**
this, that	**ce, cet, cette**
this, that	**ça**
this is	**c'est**
three	**trois**
to throw	**jeter**
Thursday	**jeudi** (m)
tip	**service** (m)
to	**à é**
to hate	**dtester**
to say	**dire**
today	**aujourd'hui**
together	**ensemble**
tomorrow	**demain**
tongue	**langue** (f)
too	**trop**
to touch	**toucher**
tower	**tour** (f)
town	**ville** (f)
trip	**tour** (m)
true	**vrai, vraie**
Tuesday	**mardi** (m)
tunnel	**tunnel** (m)
TV	**télé** (f)
twelve	**douze**
twenty	**vingt**
two	**deux**
T-shirt	**t-shirt** (m)

U

ugly	**moche**
umbrella	**parapluie** (m)
underground	**métro** (m)
to understand	**comprendre**
unite	**unité** (f)
to use	**utiliser**
useful	**utile**

V

valid	**valable**
very	**très**
video	**vidéo** (f)
video games	**jeux vidéo**
to visit	**visiter**
vocabulary	**vocabulaire** (m)

W

to wait	**attendre**
want	**avoir envie de; désirer; vouloir**
wash up	**faire la vaisselle**
washing up	**vaisselle** (f)
we	**nous**
weather	**temps** (m)
Wednesday	**mercredi** (m)
week	**semaine** (f)
weekend	**week-end** (m)
welcome	**bienvenue**
well	**alors; bien**
well done!	**bravo!**
what?	**hein?; quel? quelle?; qu'est-ce que?**
when	**quand**
where?	**où?**
whew!	**ouf!**
which?	**quel? quelle?**
white	**blanc, blanche**
who	**qui**
who is it?	**c'est qui?**
why	**pourquoi**
to win	**gagner**
wind	**vent** (m)
window	**fenêtre** (f)
winter	**hiver** (m)
with	**avec**
without	**sans**
woman	**femme** (f)
woof	**ouah**
word	**mot** (m)
to work	**travailler**
worksheet	**fiche** (f)
world	**monde** (m)
wretched	**misérable**

Y

year	**an** (m); **année** (f)
school year	**année scolaire**
I'm twelve years old	**j'ai douze ans**
yellow	**jaune**
yes	**oui**
you	**toi, tu, vous**
you don't say!	**ça alors!**
young	**jeune**
your	**ton, ta, tes, votre**
yuk!	**beurk!**
yum-yum	**miam-miam**